Mastering Python Design Patterns

Create various design patterns to master the art of solving problems using Python

Sakis Kasampalis

PUBLISHING

BIRMINGHAM - MUMBAI

Mastering Python Design Patterns

First published: January 2015

Production reference: 1220115

Published by Packt Publishing Ltd.
Livery Place
35 Livery Street
Birmingham B3 2PB, UK.

ISBN 978-1-78398-932-4

www.packtpub.com

Credits

Author

Sakis Kasampalis

Reviewers

Evan Dempsey

Amitabh Sharma

Yogendra Sharma

Patrycja Szabłowska

Commissioning Editor

Kunal Parikh

Acquisition Editor

Owen Roberts

Content Development Editor

Sumeet Sawant

Technical Editors

Tanvi Bhatt

Gaurav Suri

Copy Editors

Shivangi Chaturvedi

Nithya P.

Adithi Shetty

Project Coordinator

Aboli Ambardekar

Proofreaders

Ameesha Green

Joyce Littlejohn

Indexer

Tejal Soni

Graphics

Abhinash Sahu

Production Coordinator

Aparna Bhagat

Cover Work

Aparna Bhagat

About the Author

Sakis Kasampalis (@SKasampalis) is a software engineer living in the Netherlands. He is not dogmatic about particular programming languages and tools; his principle is that the right tool should be used for the right job. One of his favorite tools is Python because he finds it very productive.

Sakis was also the technical reviewer of *Mastering Object-oriented Python* and *Learning Python Design Patterns*, published by Packt Publishing.

I want to thank my sweetheart, Georgia, for supporting this effort. Many thanks to Owen Roberts who encouraged me to write this book. I also want to thank Sumeet Sawant for being a very kind and cooperative content development editor. Last but not least, I want to thank the reviewers of this book for their valuable feedback.

About the Reviewers

Evan Dempsey is a software developer from Waterford, Ireland. When he isn't hacking in Python for fun and profit, he enjoys craft beers, common Lisp, and keeping up with modern research in machine learning. He is a contributor to several open source projects.

Amitabh Sharma is a professional software engineer. He has worked extensively on enterprise applications in telecommunications and business analytics. His work is focused on service-oriented architecture, data warehouses, and languages such as Java, Python, and others.

I would like to thank my grandfather and my father for allowing me to learn all that I can. I would also like to thank my wife, Komal, for her support and encouragement.

Yogendra Sharma was born and brought up in a small but cultural town, Pratapgarh, in the state of Rajasthan. His basic education has been imparted in his hometown itself, and he completed his BTech in Computer Science from Jaipur. He is basically an engineer by heart and a technical enthusiast by nature.

He has vast experience in the fields of Python, Django framework, web app security, networking, Web 2.0, and C++.

Along with CCNA, many other esteemed certifications have been awarded to him. He is an active member of International Association of Engineers, Ubuntu, India, and Computer Society of India.

More recently, he participated in bug bounty programs and won many bug bounties, including the respected Yahoo, Ebay, PayPal bug bounty. He has been appointed as security researcher for several respected organizations, such as Adobe, Ebay, Avira, Moodle, Cisco, Atlassian, Basecamp, CodeClimate, Abacus, Rediff, Assembla, RecruiterBox, Tumbler, Wrike, Indeed, HybridSaaS, Sengrid, and SnapEngag.

He has reviewed many books from reputed publishing houses. You can find him on LinkedIn at `http://in.linkedin.com/in/yogendra0sharma`.

I would like to thank all my friends who always encouraged me to do something new and believing in me.

Patrycja Szabłowska is a Python developer with some Java background, with experience mainly in backend development. She graduated from Nicolaus Copernicus University in Toruń, Poland.

She is currently working in Warsaw, Poland, at Grupa Wirtualna Polska. She is constantly exploring technical novelties and is open-minded and eager to learn about the next Python library or framework. Her favorite programming motto is *Code is read much more often than it is written.*

I'd like to thank my husband, Wacław, for encouraging me to explore new frontiers, and also my parents for teaching me what matters the most.

www.PacktPub.com

Support files, eBooks, discount offers, and more

For support files and downloads related to your book, please visit www.PacktPub.com.

Did you know that Packt offers eBook versions of every book published, with PDF and ePub files available? You can upgrade to the eBook version at www.PacktPub.com and as a print book customer, you are entitled to a discount on the eBook copy. Get in touch with us at service@packtpub.com for more details.

At www.PacktPub.com, you can also read a collection of free technical articles, sign up for a range of free newsletters and receive exclusive discounts and offers on Packt books and eBooks.

https://www2.packtpub.com/books/subscription/packtlib

Do you need instant solutions to your IT questions? PacktLib is Packt's online digital book library. Here, you can search, access, and read Packt's entire library of books.

Why subscribe?

- Fully searchable across every book published by Packt
- Copy and paste, print, and bookmark content
- On demand and accessible via a web browser

Free access for Packt account holders

If you have an account with Packt at www.PacktPub.com, you can use this to access PacktLib today and view nine entirely free books. Simply use your login credentials for immediate access.

Table of Contents

Preface

Design patterns

In software engineering, a design pattern is a recommended solution to a software design problem. Design patterns generally describe how to structure our code to solve common design problems using best practices. It is important to note that a design pattern is a high-level solution; it doesn't focus on implementation details such as algorithms and data structures [GOF95, page 13], [j.mp/srcmdp]. It is up to us, as software engineers, to decide which algorithm and data structure is optimal to use for the problem we are trying to solve.

 If you are wondering what is the meaning of the text within [], please jump to the *Conventions* section of this preface for a moment to see how references are formatted in this book.

The most important part of a design pattern is probably its name. The benefit of naming all patterns is that we have, on our hands, a common vocabulary to communicate [GOF95, page 13]. Thus, if you send some code for review and your peer reviewer gives feedback mentioning *"I think that you can use a Strategy here instead of ..."*, even if you don't know or remember what a strategy is, you can immediately look it up.

As programming languages evolve, some design patterns such as Singleton become obsolete or even antipatterns [j.mp/jalfdp], others are built in the programming language (iterator), and new patterns are born (Borg/Monostate [j.mp/amdpp], [j.mp/wikidpc]).

Common misunderstandings about design patterns

There are a few misunderstandings about design patterns. One misunderstanding is that design patterns should be used right from the start when writing code. It is not unusual to see developers struggling with which pattern they should use in their code, even if they haven't first tried to solve the problem in their own way [j.mp/prsedp], [j.mp/stedp].

Not only is this wrong, but it is also against the nature of design patterns. Design patterns are discovered (in contrast to invented) as better solutions over existing solutions. If you have no existing solution, it doesn't make sense to look for a better one. Just go ahead and use your skills to solve your problem as best as you think. If your code reviewers have no objections and through time you see that your solution is smart and flexible enough, it means that you don't need to waste your time on struggling about which pattern to use. You might have even discovered a better design pattern than the existing one. Who knows? The point is do not limit your creativity in favor of forcing yourself to use existing design patterns.

A second misunderstanding is that design patterns should be used everywhere. This results in creating complex solutions with unnecessary interfaces and hierarchies, where a simpler and straightforward solution would be sufficient. Do no treat design patterns as a panacea because they are not. They must be used only if there is proof that your existing code "smells", and is hard to extend and maintain. Try thinking in terms of *you aren't gonna need it* (YAGNI [j.mp/c2yagni]) and *Keep it simple stupid* (KISS [j.mp/wikikis]). Using design patterns everywhere is as evil as premature optimization [j.mp/c2pro].

Design patterns and Python

This book focuses on design patterns in Python. Python is different than most common programming languages used in popular design patterns books (usually Java [FFBS04] or C++ [GOF95]). It supports duck-typing, functions are first-class citizens, and some patterns (for instance, iterator and decorator) are built-in features. The intent of this book is to demonstrate the most fundamental design patterns, not all patterns that have been documented so far [j.mp/wikidpc]. The code examples focus on using idiomatic Python when applicable [j.mp/idiompyt]. If you are not familiar with the Zen of Python, it is a good idea to open the Python REPL right now and execute **import this**. The Zen of Python is both amusing and meaningful.

What this book covers

Part 1: Creational patterns presents design patterns that deal with object creation.

Chapter 1, The Factory Pattern, will teach you how to use the Factory design pattern (Factory Method and Abstract Factory) to initialize objects, and cover the benefits of using the Factory design pattern instead of direct object instantiation.

Chapter 2, The Builder Pattern, will teach you how to simplify the creation of objects that are typically composed by more than one related objects.

Chapter 3, The Prototype Pattern, will teach you how to create a new object that is a full copy (hence, the name clone) of an existing object.

Part 2: Structural patterns presents design patterns that deal with relationships between the entities (classes, objects, and so on) of a system.

Chapter 4, The Adapter Pattern, will teach you how to make your existing code compatible with a foreign interface (for example, an external library) with minimal changes.

Chapter 5, The Decorator Pattern, will teach you how to enhance the functionality of an object without using inheritance.

Chapter 6, The Facade Pattern, will teach you how to create a single entry point to hide the complexity of a system.

Chapter 7, The Flyweight Pattern, will teach you how to reuse objects from an object pool to improve the memory usage and possibly the performance of your applications.

Chapter 8, The Model-View-Controller Pattern, will teach you how to improve the maintainability of your applications by avoiding mixing the business logic with the user interface.

Chapter 9, The Proxy Pattern, will teach you how to improve the security of your application by adding an extra layer of protection.

Part 3: Behavioral patterns presents design patterns that deal with the communication of the system's entities.

Chapter 10, The Chain of Responsibility Pattern, will teach you how to send a request to multiple receivers.

Chapter 11, *The Command Pattern*, will teach you how to make your application capable of reverting already applied operations.

Chapter 12, *The Interpreter Pattern*, will teach you how to create a simple language on top of Python, which can be used by domain experts without forcing them to learn how to program in Python.

Chapter 13, *The Observer Pattern*, will teach you how to send notifications to the registered stakeholders of an object whenever its state changes.

Chapter 14, *The State Pattern*, will teach you how to create a state machine to model a problem and the benefits of this technique.

Chapter 15, *The Strategy Pattern*, will teach you how to pick (during runtime) an algorithm between many available algorithms, based on some input criteria (for example, the element size).

Chapter 16, *The Template Pattern*, will teach you how to make a clear separation between the common and different parts of an algorithm to avoid unnecessary code duplication.

What you need for this book

The code is written exclusively in Python 3. Python 3 is, in many aspects, not compatible with Python 2.x [j.mp/p2orp3]. The focus is on Python 3.4.0 but using Python 3.3.0 should also be fine, since there are no syntax differences between Python 3.3.0 and Python 3.4.0 [j.mp/py3dot4]. In general, if you install the latest Python 3 version from www.python.org, you should be fine with running the examples. Most modules/libraries that are used in the examples are a part of the Python 3 distribution. If an example requires any extra modules to be installed, instructions on how to install them are given before presenting the related code.

Who this book is for

The audience of this book is Python programmers with an intermediate background and an interest in design patterns implemented in idiomatic Python. Programmers of other languages who are interested in Python can also benefit, but it's better if they first read some materials that explain how things are done in Python [j.mp/idiompyt], [j.mp/dspython].

Conventions

In this book, you will find a number of text styles that distinguish between different kinds of information. Here are some examples of these styles and an explanation of their meaning.

Code words in text, database table names, folder names, filenames, file extensions, pathnames, dummy URLs, user input, and Twitter handles are shown as follows: "We will use two libraries that are part of the Python distribution for working with XML and JSON: `xml.etree.ElementTree` and `json`."

A block of code is set as follows:

```
@property
def parsed_data(self):
    return self.data
```

When we wish to draw your attention to a particular part of a code block, the relevant lines or items are set in bold:

```
@property
def parsed_data(self):
    return self.data
```

Any command-line input or output is written as follows:

```
>>> python3 factory_method.py
```

New terms and **important words** are shown in bold. Words that you see on the screen, for example, in menus or dialog boxes, appear in the text like this: "Clicking the **Next** button moves you to the next screen."

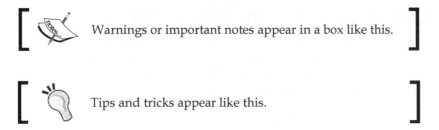

[Warnings or important notes appear in a box like this.]

[Tips and tricks appear like this.]

Book references follow the format [Author, page]. For example, the reference [GOF95, page 10] refers to the 10th page of the GOF (*Design Patterns: Elements of Reusable Object-Oriented Software*) book. At the end of the book, there is a section devoted to all book references.

Web references follow the format [j.mp/shortened]. These are shortened URL addresses that you can type or copy/paste into your web browser and be redirected to the real (usually longer and sometimes uglier) web reference. For example, typing j.mp/idiompyt in you web browser's address bar should redirect you to http://python.net/~goodger/projects/pycon/2007/idiomatic/handout.html.

Reader feedback

Feedback from our readers is always welcome. Let us know what you think about this book—what you liked or disliked. Reader feedback is important for us as it helps us develop titles that you will really get the most out of.

To send us general feedback, simply e-mail feedback@packtpub.com, and mention the book's title in the subject of your message.

If there is a topic that you have expertise in and you are interested in either writing or contributing to a book, see our author guide at www.packtpub.com/authors.

Customer support

Now that you are the proud owner of a Packt book, we have a number of things to help you to get the most from your purchase.

Downloading the example code

You can download the example code files from your account at http://www.packtpub.com for all the Packt Publishing books you have purchased. If you purchased this book elsewhere, you can visit http://www.packtpub.com/support and register to have the files e-mailed directly to you.

Errata

Although we have taken every care to ensure the accuracy of our content, mistakes do happen. If you find a mistake in one of our books—maybe a mistake in the text or the code—we would be grateful if you could report this to us. By doing so, you can save other readers from frustration and help us improve subsequent versions of this book. If you find any errata, please report them by visiting http://www.packtpub.com/submit-errata, selecting your book, clicking on the **Errata Submission Form** link, and entering the details of your errata. Once your errata are verified, your submission will be accepted and the errata will be uploaded to our website or added to any list of existing errata under the Errata section of that title.

To view the previously submitted errata, go to https://www.packtpub.com/books/content/support and enter the name of the book in the search field. The required information will appear under the **Errata** section.

Piracy

Piracy of copyrighted material on the Internet is an ongoing problem across all media. At Packt, we take the protection of our copyright and licenses very seriously. If you come across any illegal copies of our works in any form on the Internet, please provide us with the location address or website name immediately so that we can pursue a remedy.

Please contact us at copyright@packtpub.com with a link to the suspected pirated material.

We appreciate your help in protecting our authors and our ability to bring you valuable content.

Questions

If you have a problem with any aspect of this book, you can contact us at questions@packtpub.com, and we will do our best to address the problem.

1
The Factory Pattern

Creational design patterns deal with an object creation [j.mp/wikicrea]. The aim of a creational design pattern is to provide better alternatives for situations where a direct object creation (which in Python happens by the __init__() function [j.mp/divefunc], [Lott14, page 26]) is not convenient.

In the Factory design pattern, a client asks for an object without knowing where the object is coming from (that is, which class is used to generate it). The idea behind a factory is to simplify an object creation. It is easier to track which objects are created if this is done through a central function, in contrast to letting a client create objects using a direct class instantiation [Eckel08, page 187]. A factory reduces the complexity of maintaining an application by decoupling the code that creates an object from the code that uses it [Zlobin13, page 30].

Factories typically come in two forms: the **Factory Method**, which is a method (or in Pythonic terms, a function) that returns a different object per input parameter [j.mp/factorympat]; the Abstract Factory, which is a group of Factory Methods used to create a family of related products [GOF95, page 100], [j.mp/absfpat].

Factory Method

In the Factory Method, we execute a single function, passing a parameter that provides information about *what* we want. We are not required to know any details about *how* the object is implemented and *where* it is coming from.

A real-life example

An example of the Factory Method pattern used in reality is in plastic toy construction. The molding powder used to construct plastic toys is the same, but different figures can be produced using different plastic molds. This is like having a Factory Method in which the input is the name of the figure that we want (duck and car) and the output is the plastic figure that we requested. The toy construction case is shown in the following figure, which is provided by www.sourcemaking.com [j.mp/factorympat].

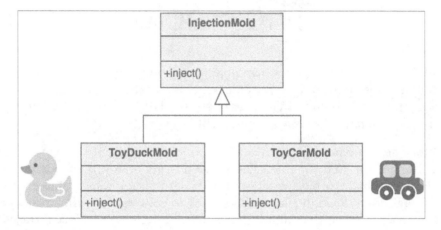

A software example

The Django framework uses the Factory Method pattern for creating the fields of a form. The forms module of Django supports the creation of different kinds of fields (CharField, EmailField) and customizations (max_length, required) [j.mp/djangofacm].

Use cases

If you realize that you cannot track the objects created by your application because the code that creates them is in many different places instead of a single function/method, you should consider using the Factory Method pattern [Eckel08, page 187]. The Factory Method centralizes an object creation and tracking your objects becomes much easier. Note that it is absolutely fine to create more than one Factory Method, and this is how it is typically done in practice. Each Factory Method logically groups the creation of objects that have similarities. For example, one Factory Method might be responsible for connecting you to different databases (MySQL, SQLite), another Factory Method might be responsible for creating the geometrical object that you request (circle, triangle), and so on.

The Factory Method is also useful when you want to decouple an object creation from an object usage. We are not coupled/bound to a specific class when creating an object, we just provide partial information about what we want by calling a function. This means that introducing changes to the function is easy without requiring any changes to the code that uses it [Zlobin13, page 30].

Another use case worth mentioning is related to improving the performance and memory usage of an application. A Factory Method can improve the performance and memory usage by creating new objects only if it is absolutely necessary [Zlobin13, page 28]. When we create objects using a direct class instantiation, extra memory is allocated every time a new object is created (unless the class uses caching internally, which is usually not the case). We can see that in practice in the following code (file id.py), it creates two instances of the same class A and uses the id() function to compare their memory addresses. The addresses are also printed in the output so that we can inspect them. The fact that the memory addresses are different means that two distinct objects are created as follows:

```python
class A(object):
    pass

if __name__ == '__main__':
    a = A()
    b = A()

    print(id(a) == id(b))
    print(a, b)
```

Executing id.py on my computer gives the following output:

```
>> python3 id.py
False
<__main__.A object at 0x7f5771de8f60> <__main__.A object at
0x7f5771df2208>
```

Note that the addresses that you see if you execute the file are not the same as I see because they depend on the current memory layout and allocation. But the result must be the same: the two addresses should be different. There's one exception that happens if you write and execute the code in the Python **Read-Eval-Print Loop (REPL)** (interactive prompt), but that's a REPL-specific optimization which is not happening normally.

Implementation

Data comes in many forms. There are two main file categories for storing/retrieving data: human-readable files and binary files. Examples of human-readable files are XML, Atom, YAML, and JSON. Examples of binary files are the `.sq3` file format used by SQLite and the `.mp3` file format used to listen to music.

In this example, we will focus on two popular human-readable formats: XML and JSON. Although human-readable files are generally slower to parse than binary files, they make data exchange, inspection, and modification much easier. For this reason, it is advised to prefer working with human-readable files, unless there are other restrictions that do not allow it (mainly unacceptable performance and proprietary binary formats).

In this problem, we have some input data stored in an XML and a JSON file, and we want to parse them and retrieve some information. At the same time, we want to centralize the client's connection to those (and all future) external services. We will use the Factory Method to solve this problem. The example focuses only on XML and JSON, but adding support for more services should be straightforward.

First, let's take a look at the data files. The XML file, `person.xml`, is based on the Wikipedia example [`j.mp/wikijson`] and contains information about individuals (`firstName`, `lastName`, `gender`, and so on) as follows:

```
<persons>
  <person>
    <firstName>John</firstName>
    <lastName>Smith</lastName>
    <age>25</age>
    <address>
      <streetAddress>21 2nd Street</streetAddress>
      <city>New York</city>
      <state>NY</state>
      <postalCode>10021</postalCode>
    </address>
    <phoneNumbers>
      <phoneNumber type="home">212 555-1234</phoneNumber>
      <phoneNumber type="fax">646 555-4567</phoneNumber>
    </phoneNumbers>
    <gender>
      <type>male</type>
    </gender>
  </person>
  <person>
    <firstName>Jimy</firstName>
```

```
      <lastName>Liar</lastName>
      <age>19</age>
      <address>
        <streetAddress>18 2nd Street</streetAddress>
        <city>New York</city>
        <state>NY</state>
        <postalCode>10021</postalCode>
      </address>
      <phoneNumbers>
        <phoneNumber type="home">212 555-1234</phoneNumber>
      </phoneNumbers>
      <gender>
        <type>male</type>
      </gender>
    </person>
    <person>
      <firstName>Patty</firstName>
      <lastName>Liar</lastName>
      <age>20</age>
      <address>
        <streetAddress>18 2nd Street</streetAddress>
        <city>New York</city>
        <state>NY</state>
        <postalCode>10021</postalCode>
      </address>
      <phoneNumbers>
        <phoneNumber type="home">212 555-1234</phoneNumber>
        <phoneNumber type="mobile">001 452-8819</phoneNumber>
      </phoneNumbers>
      <gender>
        <type>female</type>
      </gender>
    </person>
  </persons>
```

The JSON file, donut.json, comes from the GitHub account of Adobe [j.mp/adobejson] and contains donut information (type, price/unit that is, ppu, topping, and so on) as follows:

```
[
  {
    "id": "0001",
    "type": "donut",
    "name": "Cake",
    "ppu": 0.55,
```

```
    "batters": {
      "batter": [
        { "id": "1001", "type": "Regular" },
        { "id": "1002", "type": "Chocolate" },
        { "id": "1003", "type": "Blueberry" },
        { "id": "1004", "type": "Devil's Food" }
      ]
    },
    "topping": [
      { "id": "5001", "type": "None" },
      { "id": "5002", "type": "Glazed" },
      { "id": "5005", "type": "Sugar" },
      { "id": "5007", "type": "Powdered Sugar" },
      { "id": "5006", "type": "Chocolate with Sprinkles" },
      { "id": "5003", "type": "Chocolate" },
      { "id": "5004", "type": "Maple" }
    ]
  },
  {
    "id": "0002",
    "type": "donut",
    "name": "Raised",
    "ppu": 0.55,
    "batters": {
      "batter": [
        { "id": "1001", "type": "Regular" }
      ]
    },
    "topping": [
      { "id": "5001", "type": "None" },
      { "id": "5002", "type": "Glazed" },
      { "id": "5005", "type": "Sugar" },
      { "id": "5003", "type": "Chocolate" },
      { "id": "5004", "type": "Maple" }
    ]
  },
  {
    "id": "0003",
    "type": "donut",
    "name": "Old Fashioned",
    "ppu": 0.55,
    "batters": {
      "batter": [
```

```
        { "id": "1001", "type": "Regular" },
        { "id": "1002", "type": "Chocolate" }
      ]
    },
    "topping": [
      { "id": "5001", "type": "None" },
      { "id": "5002", "type": "Glazed" },
      { "id": "5003", "type": "Chocolate" },
      { "id": "5004", "type": "Maple" }
    ]
  }
]
```

We will use two libraries that are part of the Python distribution for working with XML and JSON: `xml.etree.ElementTree` and `json` as follows:

```
import xml.etree.ElementTree as etree
import json
```

The `JSONConnector` class parses the JSON file and has a `parsed_data()` method that returns all data as a dictionary (`dict`). The `property` decorator is used to make `parsed_data()` appear as a normal variable instead of a method as follows:

```
class JSONConnector:

    def __init__(self, filepath):
        self.data = dict()
        with open(filepath, mode='r', encoding='utf-8') as f:
            self.data = json.load(f)

    @property
    def parsed_data(self):
        return self.data
```

The `XMLConnector` class parses the XML file and has a `parsed_data()` method that returns all data as a list of `xml.etree.Element` as follows:

```
class XMLConnector:

    def __init__(self, filepath):
        self.tree = etree.parse(filepath)

    @property
    def parsed_data(self):
        return self.tree
```

The `connection_factory()` function is a Factory Method. It returns an instance of `JSONConnector` or `XMLConnector` depending on the extension of the input file path as follows:

```
def connection_factory(filepath):
    if filepath.endswith('json'):
        connector = JSONConnector
    elif filepath.endswith('xml'):
        connector = XMLConnector
    else:
        raise ValueError('Cannot connect to {}'.format(filepath))
    return connector(filepath)
```

The `connect_to()` function is a wrapper of `connection_factory()`. It adds exception handling as follows:

```
def connect_to(filepath):
    factory = None
    try:
        factory = connection_factory(filepath)
    except ValueError as ve:
        print(ve)
    return factory
```

The `main()` function demonstrates how the Factory Method design pattern can be used. The first part makes sure that exception handling is effective as follows:

```
def main():
    sqlite_factory = connect_to('data/person.sq3')
```

The next part shows how to work with the XML files using the Factory Method. **XPath** is used to find all `person` elements that have the last name `Liar`. For each matched person, the basic name and phone number information are shown as follows:

```
    xml_factory = connect_to('data/person.xml')
    xml_data = xml_factory.parsed_data()
    liars = xml_data.findall
    (".//{person}[{lastName}='{}']".format('Liar'))
    print('found: {} persons'.format(len(liars)))
    for liar in liars:
        print('first name:
        {}'.format(liar.find('firstName').text))
        print('last name: {}'.format(liar.find('lastName').text))
        [print('phone number ({}):'.format(p.attrib['type']),
        p.text) for p in liar.find('phoneNumbers')]
```

The final part shows how to work with the JSON files using the Factory Method. Here, there's no pattern matching, and therefore the name, price, and topping of all donuts are shown as follows:

```
json_factory = connect_to('data/donut.json')
json_data = json_factory.parsed_data
print('found: {} donuts'.format(len(json_data)))
for donut in json_data:
    print('name: {}'.format(donut['name']))
    print('price: ${}'.format(donut['ppu']))
    [print('topping: {} {}'.format(t['id'], t['type'])) for t
    in donut['topping']]
```

For completeness, here is the complete code of the Factory Method implementation (factory_method.py) as follows:

```
import xml.etree.ElementTree as etree
import json

class JSONConnector:
    def __init__(self, filepath):
        self.data = dict()
        with open(filepath, mode='r', encoding='utf-8') as f:
            self.data = json.load(f)

    @property
    def parsed_data(self):
        return self.data

class XMLConnector:
    def __init__(self, filepath):
        self.tree = etree.parse(filepath)

    @property
    def parsed_data(self):
        return self.tree

def connection_factory(filepath):
    if filepath.endswith('json'):
        connector = JSONConnector
    elif filepath.endswith('xml'):
        connector = XMLConnector
    else:
        raise ValueError('Cannot connect to {}'.format(filepath))
    return connector(filepath)
```

```python
    def connect_to(filepath):
        factory = None
        try:
            factory = connection_factory(filepath)
        except ValueError as ve:
            print(ve)
        return factory

    def main():
        sqlite_factory = connect_to('data/person.sq3')
        print()

        xml_factory = connect_to('data/person.xml')
        xml_data = xml_factory.parsed_data
        liars = xml_data.findall(".//{}[{}='{}']".format('person',
        'lastName', 'Liar'))
        print('found: {} persons'.format(len(liars)))
        for liar in liars:
            print('first name:
            {}'.format(liar.find('firstName').text))
            print('last name: {}'.format(liar.find('lastName').text))
            [print('phone number ({}):'.format(p.attrib['type']),
            p.text) for p in liar.find('phoneNumbers')]
        print()

        json_factory = connect_to('data/donut.json')
        json_data = json_factory.parsed_data
        print('found: {} donuts'.format(len(json_data)))
        for donut in json_data:
        print('name: {}'.format(donut['name']))
        print('price: ${}'.format(donut['ppu']))
        [print('topping: {} {}'.format(t['id'], t['type'])) for t
        in donut['topping']]

    if __name__ == '__main__':
        main()
```

Here is the output of this program as follows:

```
>>> python3 factory_method.py
Cannot connect to data/person.sq3

found: 2 persons
first name: Jimy
```

```
last name: Liar
phone number (home): 212 555-1234
first name: Patty
last name: Liar
phone number (home): 212 555-1234
phone number (mobile): 001 452-8819


found: 3 donuts
name: Cake
price: $0.55
topping: 5001 None
topping: 5002 Glazed
topping: 5005 Sugar
topping: 5007 Powdered Sugar
topping: 5006 Chocolate with Sprinkles
topping: 5003 Chocolate
topping: 5004 Maple
name: Raised
price: $0.55
topping: 5001 None
topping: 5002 Glazed
topping: 5005 Sugar
topping: 5003 Chocolate
topping: 5004 Maple
name: Old Fashioned
price: $0.55
topping: 5001 None
topping: 5002 Glazed
topping: 5003 Chocolate
topping: 5004 Maple
```

Notice that although JSONConnector and XMLConnector have the same interfaces, what is returned by parsed_data() is not handled in a uniform way. Different python code must be used to work with each connector. Although it would be nice to be able to use the same code for all connectors, this is at most times not realistic unless we use some kind of common mapping for the data which is very often provided by external data providers. Assuming that you can use exactly the same code for handling the XML and JSON files, what changes are required to support a third format, for example, SQLite? Find an SQLite file or create your own and try it.

As it is now, the code does not forbid a direct instantiation of a connector. Is it possible to do this? Try doing it.

> Hint: Functions in Python can have nested classes.

Abstract Factory

The Abstract Factory design pattern is a generalization of Factory Method. Basically, an Abstract Factory is a (logical) group of Factory Methods, where each Factory Method is responsible for generating a different kind of object [Eckel08, page 193].

A real-life example

Abstract Factory is used in car manufacturing. The same machinery is used for stamping the parts (doors, panels, hoods, fenders, and mirrors) of different car models. The model that is assembled by the machinery is configurable and easy to change at any time. We can see an example of the car manufacturing Abstract Factory in the following figure, which is provided by www.sourcemaking.com [j.mp/absfpat].

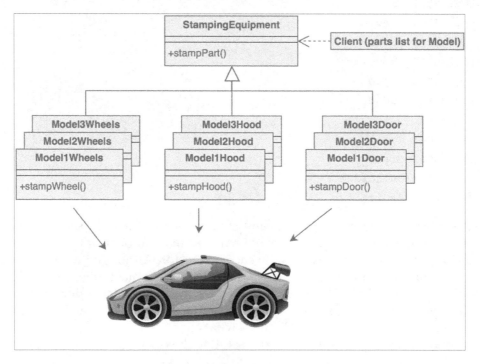

A software example

The **django_factory** package is an Abstract Factory implementation for creating Django models in tests. It is used for creating instances of models that support test-specific attributes. This is important because the tests become readable and avoid sharing unnecessary code [j.mp/djangoabs].

Use cases

Since the Abstract Factory pattern is a generalization of the Factory Method pattern, it offers the same benefits: it makes tracking an object creation easier, it decouples an object creation from an object usage, and it gives us the potential to improve the memory usage and performance of our application.

But a question is raised: how do we know when to use the Factory Method versus using an Abstract Factory? The answer is that we usually start with the Factory Method which is simpler. If we find out that our application requires many Factory Methods which it makes sense to combine for creating a family of objects, we end up with an Abstract Factory.

A benefit of the Abstract Factory that is usually not very visible from a user's point of view when using the Factory Method is that it gives us the ability to modify the behavior of our application dynamically (in runtime) by changing the active Factory Method. The classic example is giving the ability to change the look and feel of an application (for example, Apple-like, Windows-like, and so on) for the user while the application is in use, without the need to terminate it and start it again [GOF95, page 99].

Implementation

To demonstrate the Abstract Factory pattern, I will reuse one of my favorite examples, included in *Python 3 Patterns & Idioms, Bruce Eckel*, [Eckel08, page 193]. Imagine that we are creating a game or we want to include a mini-game as part of our application to entertain our users. We want to include at least two games, one for children and one for adults. We will decide which game to create and launch in runtime, based on user input. An Abstract Factory takes care of the game creation part.

Let's start with the kid's game. It is called `FrogWorld`. The main hero is a frog who enjoys eating bugs. Every hero needs a good name, and in our case the name is given by the user in runtime. The `interact_with()` method is used to describe the interaction of the frog with an obstacle (for example, bug, puzzle, and other frog) as follows:

```python
class Frog:
    def __init__(self, name):
        self.name = name

    def __str__(self):
        return self.name

    def interact_with(self, obstacle):
        print('{} the Frog encounters {} and {}!'.format(self,
        obstacle, obstacle.action()))
```

There can be many different kinds of obstacles but for our example an obstacle can only be a `Bug`. When the frog encounters a bug, only one action is supported: it eats it!

```python
class Bug:
    def __str__(self):
        return 'a bug'

    def action(self):
        return 'eats it'
```

The `FrogWorld` class is an Abstract Factory. Its main responsibilities are creating the main character and the obstacle(s) of the game. Keeping the creation methods separate and their names generic (for example, `make_character()`, `make_obstacle()`) allows us to dynamically change the active factory (and therefore the active game) without any code changes. In a statically typed language, the Abstract Factory would be an abstract class/interface with empty methods, but in Python this is not required because the types are checked in runtime [Eckel08, page 195], [j.mp/ginstromdp] as follows:

```python
class FrogWorld:
    def __init__(self, name):
        print(self)
        self.player_name = name

    def __str__(self):
        return '\n\n\t------ Frog World -------'
```

```python
    def make_character(self):
        return Frog(self.player_name)

    def make_obstacle(self):
        return Bug()
```

The `WizardWorld` game is similar. The only differences are that the wizard battles against monsters like orks instead of eating bugs!

```python
class Wizard:
    def __init__(self, name):
        self.name = name

    def __str__(self):
        return self.name

    def interact_with(self, obstacle):
        print('{} the Wizard battles against {} and
        {}!'.format(self, obstacle, obstacle.action()))

class Ork:
    def __str__(self):
        return 'an evil ork'

    def action(self):
        return 'kills it'

class WizardWorld:
    def __init__(self, name):
        print(self)
        self.player_name = name

    def __str__(self):
        return '\n\n\t------ Wizard World -------'

    def make_character(self):
        return Wizard(self.player_name)

    def make_obstacle(self):
        return Ork()
```

The GameEnvironment is the main entry point of our game. It accepts factory as an input, and uses it to create the world of the game. The play() method initiates the interaction between the created hero and the obstacle as follows:

```
class GameEnvironment:
    def __init__(self, factory):
        self.hero = factory.make_character()
        self.obstacle = factory.make_obstacle()

    def play(self):
        self.hero.interact_with(self.obstacle)
```

The validate_age() function prompts the user to give a valid age. If the age is not valid, it returns a tuple with the first element set to False. If the age is fine, the first element of the tuple is set to True and that's the case where we actually care about the second element of the tuple, which is the age given by the user as follows:

```
def validate_age(name):
    try:
        age = input('Welcome {}. How old are you? '.format(name))
        age = int(age)
    except ValueError as err:
        print("Age {} is invalid, please try
        again...".format(age))
        return (False, age)
    return (True, age)
```

Last but not least comes the main() function. It asks for the user's name and age, and decides which game should be played by the age of the user as follows:

```
def main():
    name = input("Hello. What's your name? ")
    valid_input = False
    while not valid_input:
        valid_input, age = validate_age(name)
    game = FrogWorld if age < 18 else WizardWorld
    environment = GameEnvironment(game(name))
    environment.play()
```

And the complete code of the Abstract Factory implementation (abstract_factory. py) is given as follows:

```
class Frog:
    def __init__(self, name):
        self.name = name
```

```python
    def __str__(self):
        return self.name

    def interact_with(self, obstacle):
        print('{} the Frog encounters {} and {}!'.format(self,
        obstacle, obstacle.action()))

class Bug:
    def __str__(self):
        return 'a bug'

    def action(self):
        return 'eats it'

class FrogWorld:
    def __init__(self, name):
        print(self)
        self.player_name = name

    def __str__(self):
        return '\n\n\t------ Frog World -------'

    def make_character(self):
        return Frog(self.player_name)

    def make_obstacle(self):
        return Bug()

class Wizard:
    def __init__(self, name):
        self.name = name

    def __str__(self):
        return self.name

    def interact_with(self, obstacle):
        print('{} the Wizard battles against {} and
        {}!'.format(self, obstacle, obstacle.action()))

class Ork:
    def __str__(self):
        return 'an evil ork'
```

```python
    def action(self):
        return 'kills it'

class WizardWorld:
    def __init__(self, name):
        print(self)
        self.player_name = name

    def __str__(self):
        return '\n\n\t------ Wizard World -------'

    def make_character(self):
        return Wizard(self.player_name)

    def make_obstacle(self):
        return Ork()

class GameEnvironment:
    def __init__(self, factory):
        self.hero = factory.make_character()
        self.obstacle = factory.make_obstacle()

    def play(self):
        self.hero.interact_with(self.obstacle)

def validate_age(name):
    try:
        age = input('Welcome {}. How old are you? '.format(name))
        age = int(age)
    except ValueError as err:
        print("Age {} is invalid, please try
        again...".format(age))
        return (False, age)
    return (True, age)

def main():
    name = input("Hello. What's your name? ")
    valid_input = False
    while not valid_input:
        valid_input, age = validate_age(name)
    game = FrogWorld if age < 18 else WizardWorld
    environment = GameEnvironment(game(name))
    environment.play()

if __name__ == '__main__':
    main()
```

A sample output of this program is as follows:

```
>>> python3 abstract_factory.py
Hello. What's your name? Nick
Welcome Nick. How old are you? 17
        ------ Frog World -------
Nick the Frog encounters a bug and eats it!
```

Try extending the game to make it more complete. You can go as far as you want: many obstacles, many enemies, and whatever else you like.

Summary

In this chapter, we have seen how to use the Factory Method and the Abstract Factory design patterns. Both patterns are used when we want to (a) track an object creation, (b) decouple an object creation from an object usage, or even (c) improve the performance and resource usage of an application. Case (c) was not demonstrated in the chapter. You might consider it as a good exercise.

The Factory Method design pattern is implemented as a single function that doesn't belong to any class, and is responsible for the creation of a single kind of object (a shape, a connection point, and so on). We saw how the Factory Method relates to toy construction, mentioned how it is used by Django for creating different form fields, and discussed other possible use cases for it. As an example, we implemented a Factory Method that provides access to the XML and JSON files.

The Abstract Factory design pattern is implemented as a number of Factory Methods that belong to a single class and are used to create a family of related objects (the parts of a car, the environment of a game, and so forth). We mentioned how the Abstract Factory is related with car manufacturing, how the django_factory Django package makes use of it to create clean tests, and covered the use cases of it. The implementation of the Abstract Factory is a mini-game that shows how we can use many related factories in a single class.

In the next chapter, we will talk about the Builder pattern, which is another creational pattern that can be used for fine-controlling the creation of complex objects.

2
The Builder Pattern

Imagine that we want to create an object that is composed of multiple parts and the composition needs to be done step by step. The object is not complete unless all its parts are fully created. That's where the **Builder design pattern** can help us. The Builder pattern separates the construction of a complex object from its representation. By keeping the construction separate from the representation, the same construction can be used to create several different representations [GOF95, page 110], [j.mp/builderpat].

A practical example can help us understand what the purpose of the Builder pattern is. Suppose that we want to create an HTML page generator, the basic structure (construction part) of an HTML page is always the same: it begins with <html> and finishes with </html>; inside the HTML section are the <head> and </head> elements, inside the head section are the <title> and </title> elements, and so forth. But the representation of the page can differ. Each page has its own title, its own headings, and different <body> contents. Moreover, the page is usually built in steps: one function adds the title, another adds the main heading, another the footer, and so on. Only after the whole structure of a page is complete can it be shown to the client using a final render function. We can take it even further and extend the HTML generator so that it can generate totally different HTML pages. One page might contain tables, another page might contain image galleries, yet another page contains the contact form, and so on.

The HTML page generation problem can be solved using the Builder pattern. In this pattern, there are two main participants: the **builder** and the **director**. The builder is responsible for creating the various parts of the complex object. In the HTML example, these parts are the title, heading, body, and the footer of the page. The director controls the building process using a builder instance. The HTML example means for calling the builder's functions for setting the title, the heading, and so on. Using a different builder instance allows us to create a different HTML page without touching any code of the director.

A real-life example

The Builder design pattern is used in fast-food restaurants. The same procedure is always used to prepare a burger and the packaging (box and paper bag), even if there are many different kinds of burgers (classic, cheeseburger, and more) and different packages (small-sized box, medium-sized box, and so forth). The difference between a classic burger and a cheeseburger is in the representation, and not in the construction procedure. The director is the cashier who gives instructions about what needs to be prepared to the crew, and the builder is the person from the crew that takes care of the specific order. The following figure provided by `www.sourcemaking.com` shows a **Unified Modeling Language** (**UML**) sequence diagram of the communication that takes place between the customer (client), the cashier (director), and the crew (builder) when a kid's menu is ordered [`j.mp/builderpat`].

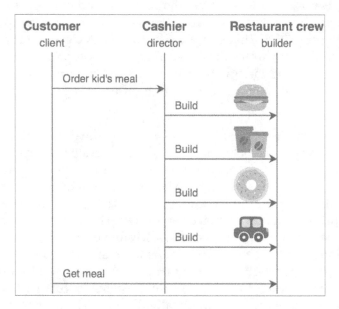

A software example

The HTML example that was mentioned at the beginning of the chapter is actually used by **django-widgy**, a third-party tree editor for Django that can be used as a **Content Management System** (**CMS**). The django-widgy editor contains a page builder that can be used for creating HTML pages with different layouts [`j.mp/widgypb`].

The **django-query-builder** library is another third-party Django library that relies on the Builder pattern. The django-query-builder library can be used for building SQL queries dynamically. Using this, we can control all aspects of a query and create a different range of queries, from simple to very complex [`j.mp/djangowidgy`].

Use cases

We use the Builder pattern when we know that an object must be created in multiple steps, and different representations of the same construction are required. These requirements exist in many applications such as page generators (like the HTML page generator mentioned in this chapter), document converters [GOF95, page 110], and **User Interface** (**UI**) form creators [j.mp/pipbuild].

Some resources mention that the Builder pattern can also be used as a solution to the telescopic constructor problem [j.mp/wikibuilder]. The telescopic constructor problem occurs when we are forced to create a new constructor for supporting different ways of creating an object. The problem is that we end up with many constructors and long parameter lists, which are hard to manage. An example of the telescopic constructor is listed at the stackoverflow website [j.mp/sobuilder]. Fortunately, this problem does not exist in Python, because it can be solved in at least two ways:

- With named parameters [j.mp/sobuipython]
- With argument list unpacking [j.mp/arglistpy]

At this point, the distinction between the Builder pattern and the Factory pattern might not be very clear. The main difference is that a Factory pattern creates an object in a single step, whereas a Builder pattern creates an object in multiple steps, and almost always through the use of a director. Some targeted implementations of the Builder pattern like Java's **StringBuilder** bypass the use of a director, but that's the exception to the rule.

Another difference is that while a Factory pattern returns a created object immediately, in the Builder pattern the client code explicitly asks the director to return the final object when it needs it [GOF95, page 113], [j.mp/builderpat].

The new computer analogy might help to distinguish between a Builder pattern and a Factory pattern. Assume that you want to buy a new computer. If you decide to buy a specific preconfigured computer model, for example, the latest Apple 1.4 GHz Mac mini, you use the Factory pattern. All the hardware specifications are already predefined by the manufacturer, who knows what to do without consulting you. The manufacturer typically receives just a single instruction. Code-wise, this would look like the following (apple-factory.py):

```
MINI14 = '1.4GHz Mac mini'

class AppleFactory:
    class MacMini14:
        def __init__(self):
            self.memory = 4 # in gigabytes
```

```
            self.hdd = 500 # in gigabytes
            self.gpu = 'Intel HD Graphics 5000'

        def __str__(self):
            info = ('Model: {}'.format(MINI14),
                    'Memory: {}GB'.format(self.memory),
                    'Hard Disk: {}GB'.format(self.hdd),
                    'Graphics Card: {}'.format(self.gpu))
            return '\n'.join(info)

    def build_computer(self, model):
        if (model == MINI14):
            return self.MacMini14()
        else:
            print("I don't know how to build {}".format(model))

if __name__ == '__main__':
    afac = AppleFactory()
    mac_mini = afac.build_computer(MINI14)
    print(mac_mini)
```

 Notice the nested `MacMini14` class. This is a neat way of forbidding the direct instantiation of a class.

Another option is buying a custom PC. In this case, you use the Builder pattern. You are the director that gives orders to the manufacturer (builder) about your ideal computer specifications. Code-wise, this looks like the following (`computer-builder.py`):

```
class Computer:
    def __init__(self, serial_number):
        self.serial = serial_number
        self.memory = None      # in gigabytes
        self.hdd = None         # in gigabytes
        self.gpu = None

    def __str__(self):
        info = ('Memory: {}GB'.format(self.memory),
                'Hard Disk: {}GB'.format(self.hdd),
                'Graphics Card: {}'.format(self.gpu))
        return '\n'.join(info)
```

```python
class ComputerBuilder:
    def __init__(self):
        self.computer = Computer('AG23385193')

    def configure_memory(self, amount):
        self.computer.memory = amount

    def configure_hdd(self, amount):
        self.computer.hdd = amount

    def configure_gpu(self, gpu_model):
        self.computer.gpu = gpu_model

class HardwareEngineer:
    def __init__(self):
        self.builder = None

    def construct_computer(self, memory, hdd, gpu):
        self.builder = ComputerBuilder()
        [step for step in (self.builder.configure_memory(memory),
                           self.builder.configure_hdd(hdd),
                           self.builder.configure_gpu(gpu))]

    @property
    def computer(self):
        return self.builder.computer

def main():
    engineer = HardwareEngineer()
    engineer.construct_computer(hdd=500, memory=8, gpu='GeForce
    GTX 650 Ti')
    computer = engineer.computer
    print(computer)

if __name__ == '__main__':
    main()
```

The basic changes are the introduction of a builder ComputerBuilder, a director HardwareEngineer, and the step-by-step construction of a computer, which now supports different configurations (notice that memory, hdd, and gpu are parameters and not preconfigured). What do we need to do if we want to support the construction of tablets? Implement this as an exercise.

You might also want to change the computer serial_number into something that is different for each computer, because as it is now it means that all computers will have the same serial number (which is impractical).

Implementation

Let's see how we can use the Builder design pattern to make a pizza ordering application. The pizza example is particularly interesting because a pizza is prepared in steps that should follow a specific order. To add the sauce, you first need to prepare the dough. To add the topping, you first need to add the sauce. And you can't start baking the pizza unless both the sauce and the topping are placed on the dough. Moreover, each pizza usually requires a different baking time, depending on the thickness of its dough and the topping used.

We start with importing the required modules and declaring a few Enum parameters [j.mp/pytenum] plus a constant that are used many times in the application. The STEP_DELAY constant is used to add a time delay between the different steps of preparing a pizza (prepare the dough, add the sauce, and so on) as follows:

```
from enum import Enum

PizzaProgress = Enum('PizzaProgress', 'queued preparation baking
ready')
PizzaDough = Enum('PizzaDough', 'thin thick')
PizzaSauce = Enum('PizzaSauce', 'tomato creme_fraiche')
PizzaTopping = Enum('PizzaTopping', 'mozzarella double_mozzarella
bacon ham mushrooms red_onion oregano')
STEP_DELAY = 3                      # in seconds for the sake of the
example
```

Our end product is a pizza, which is described by the Pizza class. When using the Builder pattern, the end product does not have many responsibilities, since it is not supposed to be instantiated directly. A builder creates an instance of the end product and makes sure that it is properly prepared. That's why the Pizza class is so minimal. It basically initializes all data to sane default values. An exception is the prepare_dough() method. The prepare_dough() method is defined in the Pizza class instead of a builder for two reasons:

- To clarify the fact that the end product is typically minimal does not mean that you should never assign it any responsibilities

- To promote code reuse through composition [GOF95, page 32]

```
class Pizza:
    def __init__(self, name):
        self.name = name
        self.dough = None
        self.sauce = None
        self.topping = []
```

```
    def __str__(self):
        return self.name

    def prepare_dough(self, dough):
        self.dough = dough
        print('preparing the {} dough of your
        {}...'.format(self.dough.name, self))
        time.sleep(STEP_DELAY)
        print('done with the {} dough'.format(self.dough.name))
```

There are two builders: one for creating a margarita pizza (MargaritaBuilder) and another for creating a creamy bacon pizza (CreamyBaconBuilder). Each builder creates a Pizza instance and contains methods that follow the pizza-making procedure: prepare_dough(), add_sauce(), add_topping(), and bake(). To be precise, prepare_dough() is just a wrapper to the prepare_dough() method of the Pizza class. Notice how each builder takes care of all the pizza-specific details. For example, the topping of the margarita pizza is double mozzarella and oregano, while the topping of the creamy bacon pizza is mozzarella, bacon, ham, mushrooms, red onion, and oregano as follows:

```
class MargaritaBuilder:
    def __init__(self):
        self.pizza = Pizza('margarita')
        self.progress = PizzaProgress.queued
        self.baking_time = 5      # in seconds for the sake of the
        example

    def prepare_dough(self):
        self.progress = PizzaProgress.preparation
        self.pizza.prepare_dough(PizzaDough.thin)

    def add_sauce(self):
        print('adding the tomato sauce to your margarita...')
        self.pizza.sauce = PizzaSauce.tomato
        time.sleep(STEP_DELAY)
        print('done with the tomato sauce')

    def add_topping(self):
        print('adding the topping (double mozzarella, oregano) to
        your margarita')
        self.pizza.topping.append([i for i in
        (PizzaTopping.double_mozzarella, PizzaTopping.oregano)])
        time.sleep(STEP_DELAY)
        print('done with the topping (double mozzarella,
        oregano)')
```

```python
    def bake(self):
        self.progress = PizzaProgress.baking
        print('baking your margarita for {}
        seconds'.format(self.baking_time))
        time.sleep(self.baking_time)
        self.progress = PizzaProgress.ready
        print('your margarita is ready')

class CreamyBaconBuilder:
    def __init__(self):
        self.pizza = Pizza('creamy bacon')
        self.progress = PizzaProgress.queued
        self.baking_time = 7      # in seconds for the sake of the
        example

    def prepare_dough(self):
        self.progress = PizzaProgress.preparation
        self.pizza.prepare_dough(PizzaDough.thick)

    def add_sauce(self):
        print('adding the crème fraîche sauce to your creamy
        bacon')

        self.pizza.sauce = PizzaSauce.creme_fraiche
        time.sleep(STEP_DELAY)

        print('done with the crème fraîche sauce')

    def add_topping(self):
        print('adding the topping (mozzarella, bacon, ham,
        mushrooms, red onion, oregano) to your creamy bacon')
        self.pizza.topping.append([t for t in
        (PizzaTopping.mozzarella, PizzaTopping.bacon,
        PizzaTopping.ham,PizzaTopping.mushrooms,
        PizzaTopping.red_onion, PizzaTopping.oregano)])
        time.sleep(STEP_DELAY)
        print('done with the topping (mozzarella, bacon, ham,
        mushrooms, red onion, oregano)')

    def bake(self):
        self.progress = PizzaProgress.baking
        print('baking your creamy bacon for {}
        seconds'.format(self.baking_time))
        time.sleep(self.baking_time)
        self.progress = PizzaProgress.ready
        print('your creamy bacon is ready')
```

The director in this example is the waiter. The core of the `Waiter` class is the `construct_pizza()` method, which accepts a builder as a parameter and executes all the pizza preparation steps in the right order. Choosing the appropriate builder, which can even be done in runtime, gives us the ability to create different pizza styles without modifying any code of the director (`Waiter`). The `Waiter` class also contains the `pizza()` method, which returns the end product (prepared pizza) as a variable to the caller as follows:

```
class Waiter:
    def __init__(self):
        self.builder = None

    def construct_pizza(self, builder):
        self.builder = builder
        [step() for step in (builder.prepare_dough,
        builder.add_sauce, builder.add_topping, builder.bake)]

    @property
    def pizza(self):
        return self.builder.pizza
```

The `validate_style()` function is similar to the `validate_age()` function as described in *Chapter 1, The Factory Pattern*. It is used to make sure that the user gives valid input, which in this case is a character that is mapped to a pizza builder. The `m` character uses the `MargaritaBuilder` class and the `c` character uses the `CreamyBaconBuilder` class. These mappings are in the builder parameter. A tuple is returned, with the first element set to `True` if the input is valid, or `False` if it is invalid as follows:

```
def validate_style(builders):
    try:
        pizza_style = input('What pizza would you like,
        [m]argarita or [c]reamy bacon? ')
        builder = builders[pizza_style]()
        valid_input = True
    except KeyError as err:
        print('Sorry, only margarita (key m) and creamy bacon (key
        c) are available')
        return (False, None)
    return (True, builder)
```

The last part is the `main()` function. The `main()` function contains a code for instantiating a pizza builder. The pizza builder is then used by the `Waiter` director for preparing the pizza. The created pizza can be delivered to the client at any later point:

```python
def main():
    builders = dict(m=MargaritaBuilder, c=CreamyBaconBuilder)
    valid_input = False
    while not valid_input:
        valid_input, builder = validate_style(builders)
    print()
    waiter = Waiter()
    waiter.construct_pizza(builder)
    pizza = waiter.pizza
    print()
    print('Enjoy your {}!'.format(pizza))
```

To put all these things together, here's the complete code of this example (`builder.py`):

```python
from enum import Enum
import time

PizzaProgress = Enum('PizzaProgress', 'queued preparation baking
ready')
PizzaDough = Enum('PizzaDough', 'thin thick')
PizzaSauce = Enum('PizzaSauce', 'tomato creme_fraiche')
PizzaTopping = Enum('PizzaTopping', 'mozzarella double_mozzarella
bacon ham mushrooms red_onion oregano')
STEP_DELAY = 3                    # in seconds for the sake of the
example

class Pizza:
    def __init__(self, name):
        self.name = name
        self.dough = None
        self.sauce = None
        self.topping = []

    def __str__(self):
        return self.name

    def prepare_dough(self, dough):
        self.dough = dough
        print('preparing the {} dough of your
        {}...'.format(self.dough.name, self))
```

```
            time.sleep(STEP_DELAY)
            print('done with the {} dough'.format(self.dough.name))

    class MargaritaBuilder:
        def __init__(self):
            self.pizza = Pizza('margarita')
            self.progress = PizzaProgress.queued
            self.baking_time = 5      # in seconds for the sake of the
            example

        def prepare_dough(self):
            self.progress = PizzaProgress.preparation
            self.pizza.prepare_dough(PizzaDough.thin)

        def add_sauce(self):
            print('adding the tomato sauce to your margarita...')
            self.pizza.sauce = PizzaSauce.tomato
            time.sleep(STEP_DELAY)
            print('done with the tomato sauce')

        def add_topping(self):
            print('adding the topping (double mozzarella, oregano) to
            your margarita')
            self.pizza.topping.append([i for i in
            (PizzaTopping.double_mozzarella, PizzaTopping.oregano)])
            time.sleep(STEP_DELAY)
            print('done with the topping (double mozzarrella,
oregano)')

        def bake(self):
            self.progress = PizzaProgress.baking
            print('baking your margarita for {}
            seconds'.format(self.baking_time))
            time.sleep(self.baking_time)
            self.progress = PizzaProgress.ready
            print('your margarita is ready')

    class CreamyBaconBuilder:
        def __init__(self):
            self.pizza = Pizza('creamy bacon')
            self.progress = PizzaProgress.queued
            self.baking_time = 7      # in seconds for the sake of the
            example
```

```python
    def prepare_dough(self):
        self.progress = PizzaProgress.preparation
        self.pizza.prepare_dough(PizzaDough.thick)

    def add_sauce(self):
        print('adding the crème fraîche sauce to your creamy
        bacon')
        self.pizza.sauce = PizzaSauce.creme_fraiche
        time.sleep(STEP_DELAY)
        print('done with the crème fraîche sauce')

    def add_topping(self):
        print('adding the topping (mozzarella, bacon, ham,
        mushrooms, red onion, oregano) to your creamy bacon')
        self.pizza.topping.append([t for t in
        (PizzaTopping.mozzarella, PizzaTopping.bacon,
        PizzaTopping.ham, PizzaTopping.mushrooms,
        PizzaTopping.red_onion, PizzaTopping.oregano)])
        time.sleep(STEP_DELAY)
        print('done with the topping (mozzarella, bacon, ham,
        mushrooms, red onion, oregano)')

    def bake(self):
        self.progress = PizzaProgress.baking
        print('baking your creamy bacon for {}
        seconds'.format(self.baking_time))
        time.sleep(self.baking_time)
        self.progress = PizzaProgress.ready
        print('your creamy bacon is ready')

class Waiter:
    def __init__(self):
        self.builder = None

    def construct_pizza(self, builder):
        self.builder = builder
        [step() for step in (builder.prepare_dough,
        builder.add_sauce, builder.add_topping, builder.bake)]

    @property
    def pizza(self):
        return self.builder.pizza
```

```
def validate_style(builders):
    try:
        pizza_style = input('What pizza would you like,
        [m]argarita or [c]reamy bacon? ')
        builder = builders[pizza_style]()
        valid_input = True
    except KeyError as err:
        print('Sorry, only margarita (key m) and creamy bacon (key
        c) are available')
        return (False, None)
    return (True, builder)

def main():
    builders = dict(m=MargaritaBuilder, c=CreamyBaconBuilder)
    valid_input = False
    while not valid_input:
        valid_input, builder = validate_style(builders)
    print()
    waiter = Waiter()
    waiter.construct_pizza(builder)
    pizza = waiter.pizza
    print()
    print('Enjoy your {}!'.format(pizza))

if __name__ == '__main__':
    main()
```

A sample output of this example is as follows:

```
>>> python3 builder.py
What pizza would you like, [m]argarita or [c]reamy bacon? r
Sorry, only margarita (key m) and creamy bacon (key c) are available
What pizza would you like, [m]argarita or [c]reamy bacon? m

preparing the thin dough of your margarita...
done with the thin dough
adding the tomato sauce to your margarita...
done with the tomato sauce
adding the topping (double mozzarella, oregano) to your margarita
done with the topping (double mozzarella, oregano)
baking your margarita for 5 seconds
your margarita is ready

Enjoy your margarita!
```

Supporting only two pizza types is a shame. Implement a Hawaiian pizza builder. Consider using inheritance after thinking about the advantages and disadvantages. Check the ingredients of a typical Hawaiian pizza and decide which class you need to extend: `MargaritaBuilder` or `CreamyBaconBuilder`? Perhaps both [j.mp/pymulti]?

In the book, *Effective Java (2nd edition)*, Joshua Bloch describes an interesting variation of the Builder pattern where calls to builder methods are chained. This is accomplished by defining the builder itself as an inner class and returning itself from each of the setter-like methods on it. The `build()` method returns the final object. This pattern is called the Fluent Builder. Here's a Python implementation, which was kindly provided by a reviewer of the book:

```python
class Pizza:
    def __init__(self, builder):
        self.garlic = builder.garlic
        self.extra_cheese  = builder.extra_cheese

    def __str__(self):
        garlic = 'yes' if self.garlic else 'no'
        cheese = 'yes' if self.extra_cheese else 'no'
        info = ('Garlic: {}'.format(garlic),
            'Extra cheese: {}'.format(cheese))
        return '\n'.join(info)

    class PizzaBuilder:
        def __init__(self):
            self.extra_cheese = False
            self.garlic = False

        def add_garlic(self):
            self.garlic = True
            return self

        def add_extra_cheese(self):
            self.extra_cheese = True
            return self

        def build(self):
            return Pizza(self)

if __name__ == '__main__':
    pizza = 
    Pizza.PizzaBuilder().add_garlic().add_extra_cheese().build()
    print(pizza)
```

Adapt the pizza example to make use of the Fluent Builder pattern. Which version of the two do you prefer? What are the pros and cons of each version?

Summary

In this chapter, we have seen how to use the Builder design pattern. We use the Builder pattern for creating an object in situations where using the Factory pattern (either a Factory Method or an Abstract Factory) is not a good option. A Builder pattern is usually a better candidate than a Factory pattern when:

- We want to create a complex object (an object composed of many parts and created in different steps that might need to follow a specific order).

- Different representations of an object are required, and we want to keep the construction of an object decoupled from its representation

- We want to create an object at one point in time but access it at a later point

We saw how the Builder pattern is used in fast-food restaurants for preparing meals, and how two third-party Django packages, django-widgy and django-query-builder, use it for generating HTML pages and dynamic SQL queries, respectively. We focused on the differences between a Builder pattern and a Factory pattern, and gave a preconfigured (Factory) versus customer (Builder) computer order analogy to clarify them.

In the implementation part, we have seen how to create a pizza ordering application, which has preparation dependencies. There are many recommended interesting exercises in this chapter, including implementing a Fluent Builder.

In the next chapter, you will learn about the last creational design pattern covered in this book: the Prototype pattern, which is used for cloning an object.

The difference between a reference and a copy is shown in the following figure:

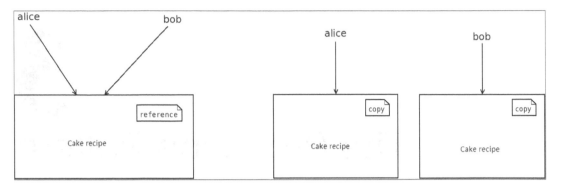

On the left part, we can see two references. Both Alice and Bob refer to the same recipe, which essentially means that they share it and all modifications are visible by both. On the right part, we can see two different copies of the same recipe. In this case, independent modifications are allowed and the changes of Alice do not affect the changes of Bob, and vice versa.

The **Prototype design pattern** helps us with creating object clones. In its simplest version, the Prototype pattern is just a `clone()` function that accepts an object as an input parameter and returns a clone of it. In Python, this can be done using the `copy.deepcopy()` function. Let's see an example. In the following code (file `clone. py`), there are two classes, A and B. A is the parent class and B is the derived class. In the main part, we create an instance of class B b, and use `deepcopy()` to create a clone of b named c. The result is that all the members of the hierarchy (at the point of time the cloning happens) are copied in the clone c. As an interesting exercise, you can try using deepcopy() with composition instead of inheritance which is shown in the following code:

```python
import copy

class A:
    def __init__(self):
        self.x = 18
        self.msg = 'Hello'

class B(A):
    def __init__(self):
        A.__init__(self)
        self.y = 34
```

```
    def __str__(self):
        return '{}, {}, {}'.format(self.x, self.msg, self.y)

if __name__ == '__main__':
    b = B()
    c = copy.deepcopy(b)
    print([str(i) for i in (b, c)])
    print([i for i in (b, c)])
```

When executing `clone.py` on my computer, I get the following:

```
>>> python3 clone.py
['18, Hello, 34', '18, Hello, 34']
[<__main__.B object at 0x7f92dac33240>, <__main__.B object at
0x7f92dac33208>]
```

Although your output of the second line will most likely not be the same as
mine, what's important is to notice that the two objects reside in two different
memory addresses (the 0x... part). This means that the two objects are two
independent copies.

In the *Implementation* section, later in this chapter, we will see how to use `copy.
deepcopy()` with some extra boilerplate code wrapped in a class, for keeping a
registry of the objects that are cloned.

A real-life example

The Prototype design pattern is all about cloning an object. Mitosis, the process
in a cell division by which the nucleus divides resulting in two new nuclei, each
of which has exactly the same chromosome and DNA content as the original cell,
is an example of biological cloning [j.mp/mmitosis].

The following figure, provided by www.sourcemaking.com, shows an example of the mitotic division of a cell [j.mp/pprotpat]:

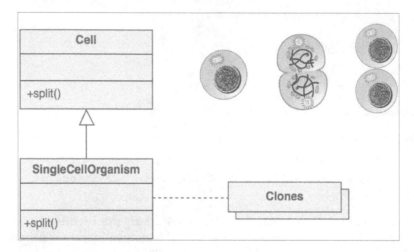

Another popular example of (artificial) cloning is Dolly, the sheep [j.mp/wikidolly].

A software example

There are many Python applications that make use of the Prototype pattern [j.mp/pythonprot], but it is almost never referred to as Prototype since cloning objects is a built-in feature of the language.

One application that uses Prototype is the **Visualization Toolkit (VTK)** [j.mp/pyvto]. VTK is an open source cross-platform system for 3D computer graphics, image processing, and visualization. VTK uses Prototype for creating clones of geometrical elements such as points, lines, hexahedrons, and so forth [j.mp/vtkcell].

Another project that uses Prototype is **music21**. According to the project's page, "music21 is a set of tools for helping scholars and other active listeners answer questions about music quickly and simply" [j.mp/pmusic21]. The music21 toolkit uses Prototype for copying musical notes and scores [j.mp/py21code].

Use cases

The Prototype pattern is useful when we have an existing object and we want to create an exact copy of it. A copy of an object is usually required when we know that parts of the object will be modified but we want to keep the original object untouched. In such cases, it doesn't make sense to recreate the original object from scratch [j.mp/protpat].

Another case where Prototype comes in handy is when we want to duplicate a complex object. By duplicating a complex object, we can think of an object that is populated from a database and has references to other objects that are also populated from a database. It is a lot of effort to create an object clone by querying the database(s) multiple times again. Using Prototype for such cases is more convenient.

So far, we have covered only the reference versus copy issue, but a copy can be further divided into a deep copy versus a shallow copy. A deep copy is what we have seen so far: all data of the original object are simply copied in the clone, without making any exceptions. A shallow copy relies on references. We can introduce data sharing, and techniques like copy-on-write to improve the performance (such as clone creation time) and the memory usage. Using shallow copies might be worthwhile if the available resources are limited (such as embedded systems) or performance is critical (such as high-performance computing).

In Python, we can do shallow copies using the `copy.copy()` function. Quoting the official Python documentation, the differences between a shallow copy (`copy.copy()`) and a deep copy (`copy.deepcopy()`) in Python are [j.mp/py3copy] as follows:

- "A *shallow copy* constructs a new compound object and then (to the extent possible) inserts *references* into it to the objects found in the original.

- A *deep copy* constructs a new compound object and then, recursively, inserts *copies* into it of the objects found in the original."

Can you think of any examples where using shallow copies is better than using deep copies?

Implementation

In programming, it is not uncommon for a book to be available in multiple editions. For example, the classic textbook on C programming *The C Programming Language* by Kernighan and Ritchie is available in two editions. The first edition was published in 1978. At that time, C was not standardized. The second edition of the book was published 10 years later and covers the standard (ANSI) version of C. What are the differences between the two editions? To mention a few, the price, the length (number of pages), and the publication date. But there are also many similarities: the authors, the publishers, and the tags/keywords that describe the book are exactly the same. This indicates that creating a new book from scratch is not always the best approach. If we know that there are many similarities between two book editions, we can use cloning and modify only the different parts of the new edition.

Let's see how we can use the Prototype pattern for creating an application that shows book information. We begin with the representation of a book. Apart from the usual initialization, the Book class demonstrates an interesting technique. It shows how we can avoid the telescopic constructor problem. In the __init__() method, only three parameters are fixed: name, authors, and price. But clients can pass more parameters in the form of keywords (name=value) using the rest variable-length list. The line self.__dict__.update(rest) adds the contents of rest to the internal dictionary of the Book class to make them part of it.

But there's a catch. Since we don't know all the names of the added parameters, we need to access the internal dict for making use of them in __str__(). And since the contents of a dictionary do not follow any specific order, we use an OrderedDict to force an order; otherwise, every time the program is executed, different outputs will be shown. Of course, you should not take my words for granted. As an exercise, remove the usage of OrderedDict and sorted() and run the example to see if I'm right:

```
class Book:
    def __init__(self, name, authors, price, **rest):
        '''Examples of rest: publisher, length, tags, publication
        date'''
        self.name = name
        self.authors = authors
        self.price = price       # in US dollars
        self.__dict__.update(rest)

    def __str__(self):
        mylist=[]
        ordered = OrderedDict(sorted(self.__dict__.items()))
        for i in ordered.keys():
            mylist.append('{}: {}'.format(i, ordered[i]))
            if i == 'price':
                mylist.append('$')
            mylist.append('\n')
        return ''.join(mylist)
```

The Prototype class implements the Prototype design pattern. The heart of the Prototype class is the clone() method, which does the actual cloning using the familiar copy.deepcopy() function. But the Prototype class does a bit more than supporting cloning. It contains the register() and unregister() methods, which can be used to keep track of the objects that are cloned in a dictionary. Note that this is just a convenience, and not a necessity.

Moreover, the `clone()` method uses the same trick that `__str__()` uses in the `Book` class, but this time for a different reason. Using the variable-length list `attr`, we can pass only the variables that really need to be modified when cloning an object as follows:

```python
class Prototype:
    def __init__(self):
        self.objects = dict()

    def register(self, identifier, obj):
        self.objects[identifier] = obj

    def unregister(self, identifier):
        del self.objects[identifier]

    def clone(self, identifier, **attr):
        found = self.objects.get(identifier)
        if not found:
            raise ValueError('Incorrect object identifier:
            {}'.format(identifier))
        obj = copy.deepcopy(found)
        obj.__dict__.update(attr)
        return obj
```

The `main()` function shows *The C Programming Language* book cloning example mentioned at the beginning of this section in practice. When cloning the first edition of the book to create the second edition, we only need to pass the modified values of the existing parameters. But we can also pass extra parameters. In this case, `edition` is a new parameter that was not needed in the first book but is useful information for the clone:

```python
def main():
    b1 = Book('The C Programming Language', ('Brian W. Kernighan',
    'Dennis M.Ritchie'), price=118, publisher='Prentice Hall',
    length=228, publication_date='1978-02-22', tags=('C',
    'programming', 'algorithms', 'data structures'))

    prototype = Prototype()
    cid = 'k&r-first'
    prototype.register(cid, b1)
    b2 = prototype.clone(cid, name='The C Programming Language
    (ANSI)', price=48.99, length=274,
    publication_date='1988-04-01', edition=2)

    for i in (b1, b2):
        print(i)
    print("ID b1 : {} != ID b2 : {}".format(id(b1), id(b2)))
```

Notice the usage of the `id()` function which returns the memory address of an object. When we clone an object using a deep copy, the memory addresses of the clone must be different from the memory addresses of the original object.

The `prototype.py` file is as follows:

```
import copy
from collections import OrderedDict


class Book:
    def __init__(self, name, authors, price, **rest):
        '''Examples of rest: publisher, length, tags, publication
        date'''
        self.name = name
        self.authors = authors
        self.price = price        # in US dollars
        self.__dict__.update(rest)

    def __str__(self):
        mylist=[]
        ordered = OrderedDict(sorted(self.__dict__.items()))
        for i in ordered.keys():
            mylist.append('{}: {}'.format(i, ordered[i]))
            if i == 'price':
                mylist.append('$')
            mylist.append('\n')
        return ''.join(mylist)

class Prototype:
    def __init__(self):
        self.objects = dict()

    def register(self, identifier, obj):
        self.objects[identifier] = obj

    def unregister(self, identifier):
        del self.objects[identifier]

    def clone(self, identifier, **attr):
        found = self.objects.get(identifier)
        if not found:
            raise ValueError('Incorrect object identifier:
            {}'.format(identifier))
        obj = copy.deepcopy(found)
```

```
            obj.__dict__.update(attr)
            return obj

    def main():
        b1 = Book('The C Programming Language', ('Brian W. Kernighan',
        'Dennis M.Ritchie'), price=118, publisher='Prentice Hall',
        length=228, publication_date='1978-02-22', tags=('C',
        'programming', 'algorithms', 'data structures'))

        prototype = Prototype()
        cid = 'k&r-first'
        prototype.register(cid, b1)
        b2 = prototype.clone(cid, name='The C Programming Language
        (ANSI)', price=48.99, length=274,
        publication_date='1988-04-01', edition=2)

        for i in (b1, b2):
            print(i)
        print("ID b1 : {} != ID b2 : {}".format(id(b1), id(b2)))

    if __name__ == '__main__':
        main()
```

The output of `id()` depends on the current memory allocation of the computer and you should expect it to differ on every execution of this program. But no matter what the actual addresses are, they should not be the same in any chance.

A sample output when I execute this program on my machine is as follows:

```
>>> python3 prototype.py
authors: ('Brian W. Kernighan', 'Dennis M. Ritchie')
length: 228
name: The C Programming Language
price: 118$
publication_date: 1978-02-22
publisher: Prentice Hall
tags: ('C', 'programming', 'algorithms', 'data structures')

authors: ('Brian W. Kernighan', 'Dennis M. Ritchie')
edition: 2
length: 274
name: The C Programming Language (ANSI)
price: 48.99$
```

```
publication_date: 1988-04-01
publisher: Prentice Hall
tags: ('C', 'programming', 'algorithms', 'data structures')


ID b1 : 140004970829304 != ID b2 : 140004970829472
```

Indeed, Prototype works as expected. The second edition of *The C Programming Language* book reuses all the information that was set in the first edition, and all the differences that we defined are only applied to the second edition. The first edition remains unaffected. Our confidence can be increased by looking at the output of the id() function: the two addresses are different.

As an exercise, you can come up with your own example of Prototype. A few ideas are as follows:

- The recipe example that was mentioned in this chapter
- The database-populated object that was mentioned in this chapter
- Copying an image so that you can add your own modifications without touching the original

Summary

In this chapter, we have seen how to use the Prototype design pattern. Prototype is used for creating exact copies of objects. Creating a copy of an object can actually mean two things:

- Relying on references, which happens when a shallow copy is created
- Duplicating everything, which happens when a deep copy is created

In the first case, we want to focus on improving the performance and the memory usage of our application by introducing data sharing between objects. But we need to be careful about modifying data, because all modifications are visible to all copies. Shallow copies were not introduced in this chapter, but you might want to experiment with them.

In the second case, we want to be able to make modifications to one copy without affecting the rest. That's useful for cases like the cake-recipe example that we have seen. Here, no data sharing is done and so we need to be careful about the resource consumption and the overhead that is introduced by our clones.

We showed a simple example of a deep copying which in Python is done using the `copy.deepcopy()` function. We also mentioned examples of cloning found in real life, focusing on mitosis.

Many software projects use Prototype, but in Python it is not mentioned as such because it is a built-in feature. Among them are the VTK, which uses Prototype for creating clones of geometrical elements, and music21, which uses it for duplicating musical scores and notes.

Finally, we discussed the use cases of Prototype and implemented a program that supports cloning books so that all information that does not change in a new edition can be reused, but at the same time modified information can be updated and new information can be added.

Prototype is the last creational design pattern covered in this book. The next chapter begins with Adapter, a structural design pattern that can be used to make two incompatible software interfaces compatible.

4

The Adapter Pattern

Structural design patterns deal with the relationships between the entities (such as classes and objects) of a system. A structural design pattern focuses on providing a simple way of composing objects for creating new functionality [GOF95, page 155], [j.mp/structpat].

Adapter is a structural design pattern that helps us make two incompatible interfaces compatible. First, let's answer what incompatible interfaces really mean. If we have an old component and we want to use it in a new system, or a new component that we want to use in an old system, the two can rarely communicate without requiring any code changes. But changing the code is not always possible, either because we don't have access to it (for example, the component is provided as an external library) or because it is impractical. In such cases, we can write an extra layer that makes all the required modifications for enabling the communication between the two interfaces. This layer is called the Adapter.

E-commerce systems are known examples. Assume that we use an e-commerce system that contains a `calculate_total(order)` function. The function calculates the total amount of an order, but only in **Danish Kroner (DKK)**. It is reasonable for our customers to ask us to add support for more popular currencies, such as **United States Dollars (USD)** and **Euros (EUR)**. If we own the source code of the system we can extend it by adding new functions for doing the conversions from DKK to USD and from DKK to EUR. But what if we don't have access to the source code of the application because it is provided to us only as an external library? In this case, we can still use the library (for example, call its methods), but we cannot modify/extend it. The solution is to write a wrapper (also known as Adapter) that converts the data from the given DKK format to the expected USD or EUR format.

The Adapter pattern is not useful only for data conversions. In general, if you want to use an interface that expects `function_a()` but you only have `function_b()`, you can use an Adapter to *convert* (adapt) `function_b()` to `function_a()` [Eckel08, page 207], [j.mp/adapterpat]. This is not only true for functions but also for function parameters. An example is a function that expects the parameters x, y, and z but you only have a function that works with the parameters x and y at hand. We will see how to use the Adapter pattern in the implementation section.

A real-life example

Probably all of us use the Adapter pattern every day, but in hardware instead of software. If you have a smartphone or a tablet, you need to use something (for example, the lightning connector of an iPhone) with a USB adapter for connecting it to your computer. If you are traveling from most European countries to the UK, you need to use a plug adapter for charging your laptop. The same is true if you are traveling from Europe to USA, or the other way around. Adapters are everywhere!

The following image, courtesy of `sourcemaking.com`, shows several examples of hardware adapters [j.mp/adapterpat]:

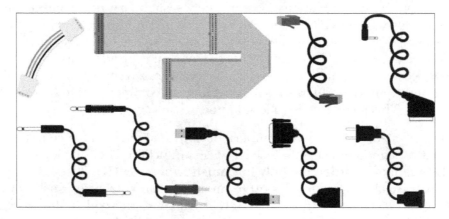

A software example

Grok is a Python framework that runs on top of Zope 3 and focuses on agile development. The Grok framework uses Adapters for making it possible for existing objects to conform to specific APIs without the need to modify them [j.mp/grokada].

The Python **Traits** package also uses the Adapter pattern for transforming an object that does not implement of a specific interface (or set of interfaces) to an object that does [j.mp/pytraitsad].

Use cases

The Adapter pattern is used for making things work after they have been implemented [j.mp/adapterpat]. Usually one of the two incompatible interfaces is either foreign or old/legacy. If the interface is foreign, it means that we have no access to the source code. If it is old it is usually impractical to refactor it. We can take it even further and argue that altering the implementation of a legacy component to meet our needs is not only impractical, but it also violates the open/close principle [j.mp/adaptsimp]. The **open/close principle** is one of the fundamental principles of Object-Oriented design (the O of SOLID). It states that a software entity should be open for extension, but closed for modification. That basically means that we should be able to extend the behavior of an entity without making source code modifications. Adapter respects the open/closed principle [j.mp/openclosedp].

Therefore, using an Adapter for making things work after they have been implemented is a better approach because it:

- Does not require access to the source code of the foreign interface
- Does not violate the open/closed principle

Implementation

There are many ways of implementing the Adapter design pattern in Python [Eckel08, page 207]. All the techniques demonstrated by *Bruce Eckel* use inheritance, but Python provides an alternative, and in my opinion, a more idiomatic way of implementing an Adapter. The alternative technique should be familiar to you, since it uses the internal dictionary of a class, and we have seen how to do that in *Chapter 3, The Prototype Pattern*.

Let's begin with the *what we have* part. Our application has a Computer class that shows basic information about a computer. All the classes of this example, including the Computer class are very primitive, because we want to focus on the Adapter pattern and not on how to make a class as complete as possible.

```python
class Computer:
    def __init__(self, name):
        self.name = name

    def __str__(self):
        return 'the {} computer'.format(self.name)

    def execute(self):
        return 'executes a program'
```

In this case, the execute() method is the main action that the computer can perform. This method is called by the client code.

Now we move to the *what we want* part. We decide to enrich our application with more functionality, and luckily, we find two interesting classes implemented in two different libraries that are unrelated with our application: Synthesizer and Human. In the Synthesizer class, the main action is performed by the play() method. In the Human class, it is performed by the speak() method. To indicate that the two classes are external, we place them in a separate module, as shown:

```
class Synthesizer:
    def __init__(self, name):
        self.name = name

    def __str__(self):
        return 'the {} synthesizer'.format(self.name)

    def play(self):
        return 'is playing an electronic song'

class Human:
    def __init__(self, name):
        self.name = name

    def __str__(self):
        return '{} the human'.format(self.name)

    def speak(self):
        return 'says hello'
```

So far so good. But, we have a problem. The client only knows how to call the execute() method, and it has no idea about play() or speak(). How can we make the code work without changing the Synthesizer and Human classes? Adapters to the rescue! We create a generic Adapter class that allows us to adapt a number of objects with different interfaces, into one unified interface. The obj argument of the __init__() method is the object that we want to adapt, and adapted_methods is a dictionary containing key/value pairs of method the client calls/method that should be called.

```
class Adapter:
    def __init__(self, obj, adapted_methods):
        self.obj = obj
        self.__dict__.update(adapted_methods)

    def __str__(self):
        return str(self.obj)
```

Let's see how we can use the Adapter pattern. An `objects` list holds all the objects. The compatible objects that belong to the `Computer` class need no adaptation. We can add them directly to the list. The incompatible objects are not added directly. They are adapted using the `Adapter` class. The result is that the client code can continue using the known `execute()` method on all objects without the need to be aware of any interface differences between the used classes.

```python
def main():
    objects = [Computer('Asus')]
    synth = Synthesizer('moog')
    objects.append(Adapter(synth, dict(execute=synth.play)))
    human = Human('Bob')
    objects.append(Adapter(human, dict(execute=human.speak)))

    for i in objects:
        print('{} {}'.format(str(i), i.execute()))
```

Let's see the complete code of the Adapter pattern example (files `external.py` and `adapter.py`) as follows:

```python
class Synthesizer:
    def __init__(self, name):
        self.name = name

    def __str__(self):
        return 'the {} synthesizer'.format(self.name)

    def play(self):
        return 'is playing an electronic song'

class Human:
    def __init__(self, name):
        self.name = name

    def __str__(self):
        return '{} the human'.format(self.name)

    def speak(self):
        return 'says hello'

from external import Synthesizer, Human

class Computer:
    def __init__(self, name):
        self.name = name
```

```
        def __str__(self):
            return 'the {} computer'.format(self.name)

        def execute(self):
            return 'executes a program'

    class Adapter:
        def __init__(self, obj, adapted_methods):
            self.obj = obj
            self.__dict__.update(adapted_methods)

        def __str__(self):
            return str(self.obj)


    def main():
        objects = [Computer('Asus')]
        synth = Synthesizer('moog')
        objects.append(Adapter(synth, dict(execute=synth.play)))
        human = Human('Bob')
        objects.append(Adapter(human, dict(execute=human.speak)))

        for i in objects:
            print('{} {}'.format(str(i), i.execute()))

    if __name__ == "__main__":
        main()
```

The output when executing the example is:

```
>>> python3 adapter.py
the Asus computer executes a program
the moog synthesizer is playing an electronic song
Bob the human says hello
```

We managed to make the Human and Synthesizer classes compatible with the interface expected by the client, without changing their source code. This is nice.

Here's a challenging exercise for you. There is a problem with this implementation. While all classes have a name attribute, the following code fails:

```
    for i in objects:
        print(i.name)
```

First of all, why does this code fail? Although this makes sense from a coding point of view, it does not make sense at all for the client code which should not be aware of details such as what is adapted and what is not adapted. We just want to provide a uniform interface. How can we make this code work?

 Hint: Think of how you can delegate the non-adapted parts to the object contained in the Adapter class.

Summary

This chapter covered the Adapter design pattern. We use the Adapter pattern for making two (or more) incompatible interfaces compatible. As a motivation, an e-commerce system that should support multiple currencies was mentioned. We use adapters every day for interconnecting devices, charging them, and so on.

Adapter makes things work after they have been implemented. The Grok Python framework and the Traits package use the Adapter pattern for achieving API conformance and interface compatibility, respectively. The open/close principle is strongly connected with these aspects.

In the implementation section, we saw how to achieve interface conformance using the Adapter pattern without modifying the source code of the incompatible model. This is achieved through a generic Adapter class that does the work for us. Although we could use sub-classing (inheritance) to implement the Adapter pattern in the traditional way in Python, this technique is a great alternative.

In the next chapter, we will see how we can use the Decorator pattern to extend the behavior of an object without using sub-classing.

5

The Decorator Pattern

Whenever we want to add extra functionality to an object, we have a number of different options. We can:

- Add the functionality directly to the class the object belongs to, if it makes sense (for example, add a new method)
- Use composition
- Use inheritance

Composition should generally be preferred over inheritance, because inheritance makes code reuse harder, it's static, and applies to an entire class and all instances of it [GOF95, page 31], [j.mp/decopat].

Design patterns offer us a fourth option that supports extending the functionality of an object dynamically (in runtime): Decorators. A **Decorator** pattern can add responsibilities to an object dynamically, and in a transparent manner (without affecting other objects) [GOF95, page 196].

In many programming languages, the Decorator pattern is implemented using sub-classing (inheritance) [GOF95, page 198]. In Python, we can (and should) use the built-in decorator feature. A Python decorator is a specific change to the syntax of Python that is used for extending the behavior of a class, method, or function without using inheritance. In terms of implementation, a Python decorator is a callable (function, method, class) that accepts a function object fin as input, and returns another function object fout [j.mp/conqdec]. This means that any callable that has these properties can be treated as a decorator. We have already seen how to use the built-in property decorator that makes a method appear as a variable in *Chapter 1*, *The Factory Pattern* and *Chapter 2*, *The Builder Pattern*. In the implementation section, we will learn how to implement and use our own decorators.

There is no one-to-one relationship between the Decorator pattern and Python decorators. Python decorators can actually do much more than the Decorator pattern. One of the things they can be used for, is to implement the Decorator pattern [Eckel08, page 59], [j.mp/moinpydec].

A real-life example

The fact that the pattern is called Decorator does not mean that it should be used only for making things look prettier. The Decorator pattern is generally used for extending the functionality of an object. Real examples of such extensions are: adding a silencer to a gun, using different camera lenses (in cameras with removable lenses), and so on.

The following figure, provided by sourcemaking.com, shows how we can *decorate* a gun with special accessories to make it silent, more accurate, and devastating [j.mp/decopat]. Note that the figure uses sub-classing, but in Python, this is not necessary because we can use the built-in decorator feature of the language.

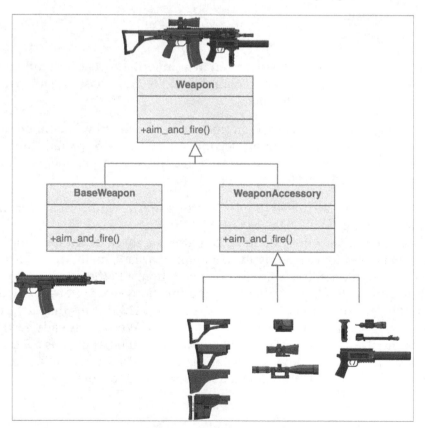

A software example

The Django framework uses decorators to a great extent. An example is the View decorator. Django's **View** decorators can be used for [j.mp/djangodec]:

- Restricting access to views based on the HTTP request
- Controlling the caching behavior on specific views
- Controlling compression on a per-view basis
- Controlling caching based on specific HTTP request headers

The Grok framework also uses decorators for achieving different goals such as [j.mp/grokdeco]:

- Registering a function as an event subscriber
- Protecting a method with a specific permission
- Implementing the Adapter pattern

Use cases

The Decorator pattern shines when used for implementing **cross-cutting concerns** [Lott14, page 223], [j.mp/wikicrosscut]. Examples of cross-cutting concerns are:

- Data validation
- Transaction processing (A transaction in this case is similar to a database transaction, in the sense that either all steps should be completed successfully, or the transaction should fail.)
- Caching
- Logging
- Monitoring
- Debugging
- Business rules
- Compression
- Encryption

In general, all parts of an application that are generic and can be applied to many other parts of it, are considered cross-cutting concerns.

Another popular example of using the Decorator pattern is **Graphical User Interface (GUI)** toolkits. In a GUI toolkit, we want to be able to add features such as borders, shadows, colors, and scrolling to individual components/widgets [GOF95, page 196].

Implementation

Python decorators are generic and very powerful. You can find many examples of how they can be used at the decorator library of python.org [j.mp/pydeclib]. In this section, we will see how we can implement a **memoization** decorator [j.mp/memoi]. All recursive functions can benefit from memoization, so let's pick the popular Fibonacci sequence example. Implementing the recursive algorithm of Fibonacci is straight forward, but it has major performance issues, even for small values. First, let's see the naive implementation (file fibonacci_naive.py).

```
def fibonacci(n):
    assert(n >= 0), 'n must be >= 0'
    return n if n in (0, 1) else fibonacci(n-1) + fibonacci(n-2)


if __name__ == '__main__':
    from timeit import Timer
    t = Timer('fibonacci(8)', 'from __main__ import fibonacci')
    print(t.timeit())
```

A sample execution of this example shows how slow this implementation is. It takes 17 seconds to calculate the eighth Fibonacci number. The same execution gives the following output:

```
>>> python3 fibonacci_naive.py
16.669270177000726
```

Let's use memoization to see if it helps. In the following code, we use a dict for caching the already computed values of the Fibonacci sequence. We also change the parameter passed to the fibonacci() function. We want to calculate the hundredth Fibonacci number instead of the eighth.

```
known = {0:0, 1:1}

def fibonacci(n):
    assert(n >= 0), 'n must be >= 0'
    if n in known:
        return known[n]
    res = fibonacci(n-1) + fibonacci(n-2)
    known[n] = res
```

```
        return res

if __name__ == '__main__':
    from timeit import Timer
    t = Timer('fibonacci(100)', 'from __main__ import fibonacci')
    print(t.timeit())
```

Executing the memoization-based code shows that performance improves dramatically, and is acceptable even for computing large values. A sample execution is as follows:

```
>>> python3 fibonacci.py
0.31532211999729043
```

But there are already a few problems with this approach. While the performance is not an issue any longer, the code is not as clean as it is when not using memoization. And what happens if we decide to extend the code with more math functions and turn it into a module? Let's assume that the next function we decide to add is nsum(), which returns the sum of the first n numbers. Note that this function is already available in the math module as fsum(), but we can easily think of other functions that are not available in the standard library and would be useful for our module (for example Pascal's triangle, the sieve of Eratosthenes, and so on). The code of the nsum() function using memoization (file mymath.py) is given as follows:

```
known_sum = {0:0}

def nsum(n):
    assert(n >= 0), 'n must be >= 0'
    if n in known_sum:
        return known_sum[n]
    res = n + nsum(n-1)
    known_sum[n] = res
    return res
```

Do you notice the problem already? We ended up with a new dict called known_sum which acts as our cache for nsum, and a function that is more complex than it would be without using memoization. Our module is becoming unnecessarily complex. Is it possible to keep the recursive functions as simple as the naive versions, but achieve a performance similar to the performance of the functions that use memoization? Fortunately, it is, and the solution is to use the Decorator pattern.

First, we create a `memoize()` decorator as shown in the following example. Our decorator accepts the function `fn` that needs to be memoized, as an input. It uses a `dict` named `known` as the cache. The `functools.wraps()` function is a function that is used for convenience when creating decorators. It is not mandatory but a good practice to use since it makes sure that the documentation and the signature of the function that is decorated, are preserved [`j.mp/funcwraps`]. The argument list `*args`, is required in this case because the functions that we want to decorate accept input arguments. It would be redundant to use it if `fibonacci()` and `nsum()` didn't require any arguments, but they require `n`.

```python
import functools

def memoize(fn):
    known = dict()

    @functools.wraps(fn)
    def memoizer(*args):
        if args not in known:
            known[args] = fn(*args)
        return known[args]

    return memoizer
```

Now, we can use our `memoize()` decorator with the naive version of our functions. This has the benefit of readable code without performance impacts. We apply a decorator using what is known as decoration (or decoration line). A decoration uses the `@name` syntax, where `name` is the name of the decorator that we want to use. It is nothing more than syntactic sugar for simplifying the usage of decorators. We can even bypass this syntax and execute our decorator manually, but that is left as an exercise for you. Let's see how the `memoize()` decorator is used with our recursive functions in the following example:

```python
@memoize
def nsum(n):
    '''Returns the sum of the first n numbers'''
    assert(n >= 0), 'n must be >= 0'
    return 0 if n == 0 else n + nsum(n-1)

@memoize
def fibonacci(n):
    '''Returns the nth number of the Fibonacci sequence'''
    assert(n >= 0), 'n must be >= 0'
    return n if n in (0, 1) else fibonacci(n-1) + fibonacci(n-2)
```

The last part of the code shows how to use the decorated functions and measure their performance. `measure` is a `list` of `dict` used to avoid code repetition. Note how `__name__` and `__doc__` show the proper function names and documentation values, respectively. Try removing the `@functools.wraps(fn)` decoration from `memoize()`, and see if this is still the case:

```
if __name__ == '__main__':
    from timeit import Timer
    measure = [ {'exec':'fibonacci(100)', 'import':'fibonacci',
    'func':fibonacci},{'exec':'nsum(200)', 'import':'nsum',
    'func':nsum} ]
    for m in measure:
        t = Timer('{}'.format(m['exec']), 'from __main__ import
        {}'.format(m['import']))
        print('name: {}, doc: {}, executing: {}, time:
        {}'.format(m['func'].__name__, m['func'].__doc__,
        m['exec'], t.timeit()))
```

Let's see the complete code of our math module (file `mymath.py`) and a sample output when executing it.

```
import functools

def memoize(fn):
    known = dict()

    @functools.wraps(fn)
    def memoizer(*args):
        if args not in known:
            known[args] = fn(*args)
        return known[args]

    return memoizer

@memoize
def nsum(n):
    '''Returns the sum of the first n numbers'''
    assert(n >= 0), 'n must be >= 0'
    return 0 if n == 0 else n + nsum(n-1)

@memoize
def fibonacci(n):
    '''Returns the nth number of the Fibonacci sequence'''
    assert(n >= 0), 'n must be >= 0'
    return n if n in (0, 1) else fibonacci(n-1) + fibonacci(n-2)
```

```
if __name__ == '__main__':
    from timeit import Timer
    measure = [ {'exec':'fibonacci(100)', 'import':'fibonacci',
    'func':fibonacci}, {'exec':'nsum(200)', 'import':'nsum',
    'func':nsum} ]
    for m in measure:
        t = Timer('{}'.format(m['exec']), 'from __main__
        import{}'.format(m['import']))
        print('name: {}, doc: {}, executing: {}, time:
        {}'.format(m['func'].__name__, m['func'].__doc__,
        m['exec'], t.timeit()))
```

Note that the execution times might differ in your case.

```
>>> python3 mymath.py
```

```
name: fibonacci, doc: Returns the nth number of the Fibonacci
sequence, executing: fibonacci(100), time: 0.4169441329995607
```

```
name: nsum, doc: Returns the sum of the first n numbers,
executing: nsum(200), time: 0.4160157349997462
```

Nice. Readable code and acceptable performance. Now, you might argue that this is not the Decorator pattern, since we don't apply it in runtime. The truth is that a decorated function cannot be undecorated; but you can still decide in runtime if the decorator will be executed or not. That's an interesting exercise left for you.

 Hint: Use a decorator that acts as a wrapper which decides whether or not the *real* decorator is executed based on some condition.

Another interesting property of decorators that is not covered in this chapter is that, you can decorate a function with more than one decorator. So here's another exercise: create a decorator that helps you to debug recursive functions, and apply it on nsum() and fibonacci(). In what order are the multiple decorators executed?

If you have not had enough with decorators, I have one last exercise for you. The memoize() decorator does not work with functions that accept more than one argument. How can we verify that? After verifying it, try finding a way of fixing this issue.

Summary

This chapter covered the Decorator pattern and its relation to the Python programming language. We use the Decorator pattern as a convenient way of extending the behavior of an object without using inheritance. Python extends the Decorator concept even more, by allowing us to extend the behavior of any callable (function, method, or class) without using inheritance or composition. We can use the built-in decorator feature of Python.

We have seen a few examples of objects that are decorated in reality, like guns and cameras. From a software point of view, both Django and Grok use decorators for achieving different goals, such as controlling HTTP compression and caching.

The Decorator pattern is a great solution for implementing cross-cutting concerns, because they are generic and do not fit well into the OOP paradigm. We mentioned many categories of cross-cutting concerns in the *Use cases* section. In fact, in the *Implementation* section a cross-cutting concern was demonstrated: memoization. We saw how decorators can help us to keep our functions clean, without sacrificing performance.

The recommended exercises in this chapter can help you understand decorators even better, so that you can use this very powerful tool for solving many common (and perhaps less common) programming problems. The next chapter covers the Facade pattern, which is a convenient way of simplifying access to a complex system.

6
The Facade Pattern

As systems evolve, they can get very complex. It is not unusual to end up with a very large (and sometimes confusing) collection of classes and interactions. In many cases, we don't want to expose this complexity to the client. The Facade (also known as Façade) design pattern helps us to hide the internal complexity of our systems and expose only what is necessary to the client through a simplified interface [Eckel08, page 209]. In essence, **Facade** is an abstraction layer implemented over an existing complex system.

The role of Facade is demonstrated in the following figure. The figure is a class diagram representation of Wikipedia's Java Facade example [j.mp/wikifac]. A computer is a complex machine that depends on several parts to be fully functional. To keep things simple, the word *computer* in this case, refers to an IBM derivative that uses a Von Neumann architecture. Booting a computer is a particularly complex procedure. The CPU, main memory, and hard disk need to be up and running; the boot loader must be loaded from the hard disk to the main memory, the CPU must boot the operating system kernel, and so forth. Instead of exposing all this complexity to the client, we create a Facade that encapsulates the whole procedure, making sure that all steps are executed in the right order.

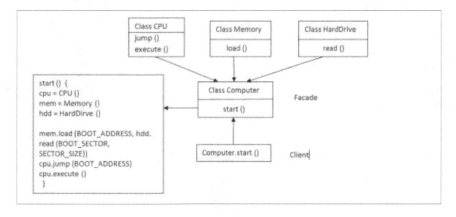

From the classes shown in the figure, only the `Computer` class needs to be exposed to the client code. The client executes only the `start()` method of `Computer`. All the other complex parts are taken care of by the Facade `Computer` class.

A real-life example

The Facade pattern is quite common in reality. When you call a bank or company, you are usually first connected to the customer service department. The customer service employee acts as a Facade between you and the actual department (billing, technical support, general assistance, and so on) and the employee that will help you with your specific problem. The following figure, provided by `sourcemaking.com`, shows this example graphically [`j.mp/facadepat`]:

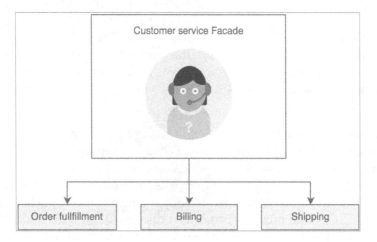

A key used to turn on a car or motorcycle can also be considered a Facade. It is a simple way of activating a system that is very complex internally. And of course, the same is true for other complex electronic devices that we can activate with a single button, such as computers.

A software example

The **django-oscar-datacash** module is a Django third-party module that integrates with the **DataCash** payment gateway. The module has a `Gateway` class that provides fine-grained access to the various DataCash APIs. On top of that, it also offers a `Facade` class that provides a less granular API (for those who don't want to mess with the details) and the ability to save transactions for auditing purposes [`j.mp/oscarfac`].

Caliendo, an interface for mocking Python APIs, contains a `facade` module which uses the Facade pattern for doing many different but useful things, such as caching methods and deciding what to return based on the input object which is passed to the top-level `Facade` method [j.mp/caliendofac].

Use cases

The most usual reason to use the Facade pattern is for providing a single, simple entry point to a complex system. By introducing Facade, the client code can use a system by simply calling a single method/function. At the same time, the internal system does not lose any functionality. It just encapsulates it.

Not exposing the internal functionality of a system to the client code gives us an extra benefit; we can introduce changes to the system, but the client code remains unaware and unaffected by the changes. No modifications are required to the client code [Zlobin13, page 44].

Facade is also useful if you have more than one layer in your system. You can introduce one Facade entry point per layer, and let all layers communicate with each other through their Facades. That promotes loose coupling and keeps the layers as independent as possible [GOF95, page 209].

Implementation

Assume that we want to create an operating system using a multi-server approach, similar to how it is done in MINIX 3 [j.mp/minix3] or GNU Hurd [j.mp/gnuhurd]. A multi-server operating system has a minimal kernel, called the **microkernel**, that runs in privileged mode. All the other services of the system are following a server architecture (driver server, process server, file server, and so forth). Each server belongs to a different memory address space and runs on top of the microkernel in user mode. The pros of this approach are that the operating system can become more fault-tolerant, reliable, and secure. For example, since all drivers are running in user mode on a driver server, a bug in a driver cannot crash the whole system, and neither can it affect the other servers. The cons of this approach are the performance overhead and the complexity of system programming, because the communication between a server and the microkernel, as well as between the independent servers, happens using message passing. Message passing is more complex than the shared memory model used in monolithic kernels like Linux [j.mp/helenosm].

We begin with a `Server` interface. An `Enum` parameter describes the different possible states of a server. We use the `abc` module to forbid direct instantiation of the `Server` interface and make the fundamental `boot()` and `kill()` methods mandatory, assuming that different actions are needed to be taken for booting, killing, and restarting each server. If you have not used the `abc` module before, note the following important things:

- We need to subclass `ABCMeta`, using the `metaclass` keyword
- We use the `@abstractmethod` decorator for stating which methods should be implemented (mandatory) by all subclasses of `Server`

Try removing the `boot()` or `kill()` method of a subclass and see what happens. Do the same after removing the `@abstractmethod` decorator also. Do things work as you expected?

Let's consider the following code:

```python
State = Enum('State', 'new running sleeping restart zombie')

class Server(metaclass=ABCMeta):
    @abstractmethod
    def __init__(self):
        pass

    def __str__(self):
        return self.name

    @abstractmethod
    def boot(self):
        pass

    @abstractmethod
    def kill(self, restart=True):
        pass
```

A modular operating system can have a great number of interesting servers: a file server, a process server, an authentication server, a network server, a graphical/window server, and so forth. The following example includes two stub servers-the `FileServer`, and the `ProcessServer`. Apart from the methods required to be implemented by the `Server` interface, each server can have its own specific methods. For instance the `FileServer` has a `create_file()` method for creating files, and the `ProcessServer` has a `create_process()` method for creating processes.

```python
class FileServer(Server):
    def __init__(self):
        '''actions required for initializing the file server'''
```

```python
        self.name = 'FileServer'
        self.state = State.new

    def boot(self):
        print('booting the {}'.format(self))
        '''actions required for booting the file server'''
        self.state = State.running

def kill(self, restart=True):
        print('Killing {}'.format(self))
        '''actions required for killing the file server'''
        self.state = State.restart if restart else State.zombie

    def create_file(self, user, name, permissions):
        '''check validity of permissions, user rights, etc.'''

        print("trying to create the file '{}' for user '{}' with
        permissions {}".format(name, user, permissions))

class ProcessServer(Server):
    def __init__(self):
        '''actions required for initializing the process server'''
        self.name = 'ProcessServer'
        self.state = State.new

    def boot(self):
        print('booting the {}'.format(self))
        '''actions required for booting the process server'''
        self.state = State.running

    def kill(self, restart=True):
        print('Killing {}'.format(self))
        '''actions required for killing the process server'''
        self.state = State.restart if restart else State.zombie

    def create_process(self, user, name):
        '''check user rights, generate PID, etc.'''

        print("trying to create the process '{}' for user
        '{}'".format(name, user))
```

The OperatingSystem class is a Facade. In __init__(), all the necessary server instances are created. The start() method, used by the client code, is the entry point to the system. More wrapper methods can be added, if necessary, as access point to the services of the servers such as the wrappers create_file() and create_process(). From the client's point of view, all those services are provided by the OperatingSystem class. The client should not be confused with unnecessary details such as the existence of servers and the responsibility of each server.

```python
class OperatingSystem:
    '''The Facade'''
    def __init__(self):
        self.fs = FileServer()
        self.ps = ProcessServer()

    def start(self):
        [i.boot() for i in (self.fs, self.ps)]

    def create_file(self, user, name, permissions):
        return self.fs.create_file(user, name, permissions)

    def create_process(self, user, name):
        return self.ps.create_process(user, name)
```

In the following full code listing (file facade.py), you can see that there are many dummy classes and servers. They are there to give an idea about the required abstractions (User, Process, File, and so forth) and servers (WindowServer, NetworkServer, and so forth) for making the system functional. A recommended exercise is to implement at least one service of the system (for example, file creation). Feel free to change the interface and the signature of the methods to fit your needs. Make sure that after your changes, the client code does not need to know anything other than the Facade OperatingSystem class:

```python
from enum import Enum
from abc import ABCMeta, abstractmethod

State = Enum('State', 'new running sleeping restart zombie')

class User:
    pass

class Process:
    pass

class File:
    pass
```

```python
class Server(metaclass=ABCMeta):
    @abstractmethod
    def __init__(self):
        pass

    def __str__(self):
        return self.name

    @abstractmethod
    def boot(self):
        pass

    @abstractmethod
    def kill(self, restart=True):
        pass

class FileServer(Server):
    def __init__(self):
        '''actions required for initializing the file server'''
        self.name = 'FileServer'
        self.state = State.new

    def boot(self):
        print('booting the {}'.format(self))
        '''actions required for booting the file server'''
        self.state = State.running

    def kill(self, restart=True):
        print('Killing {}'.format(self))
        '''actions required for killing the file server'''
        self.state = State.restart if restart else State.zombie

    def create_file(self, user, name, permissions):
        '''check validity of permissions, user rights, etc.'''

        print("trying to create the file '{}' for user '{}' with
        permissions {}".format(name, user, permissions))

class ProcessServer(Server):
    def __init__(self):
        '''actions required for initializing the process server'''
        self.name = 'ProcessServer'
        self.state = State.new
```

```python
    def boot(self):
        print('booting the {}'.format(self))
        '''actions required for booting the process server'''
        self.state = State.running

    def kill(self, restart=True):
        print('Killing {}'.format(self))
        '''actions required for killing the process server'''
        self.state = State.restart if restart else State.zombie

    def create_process(self, user, name):
        '''check user rights, generate PID, etc.'''

        print("trying to create the process '{}' for user
        '{}'".format(name, user))

class WindowServer:
    pass

class NetworkServer:
    pass

class OperatingSystem:
    '''The Facade'''
    def __init__(self):
        self.fs = FileServer()
        self.ps = ProcessServer()

    def start(self):
        [i.boot() for i in (self.fs, self.ps)]

    def create_file(self, user, name, permissions):
        return self.fs.create_file(user, name, permissions)

    def create_process(self, user, name):
        return self.ps.create_process(user, name)

def main():
    os = OperatingSystem()
    os.start()
    os.create_file('foo', 'hello', '-rw-r-r')
    os.create_process('bar', 'ls /tmp')

if __name__ == '__main__':
    main()
```

Executing the example shows the starting message of our two stub servers:

```
>>> python3 facade.py
booting the FileServer
booting the ProcessServer
trying to create the file 'hello' for user 'foo' with permissions -
rw-r-r
trying to create the process 'ls /tmp' for user 'bar'
```

The Facade `OperatingSystem` class does a good job. The client code can create files and processes without needing to know internal details about the operating system, such as the existence of multiple servers. To be precise, the client code can call the methods for creating files and processes, but they are currently dummy. As an interesting exercise, you can implement one of the two methods, or even both.

Summary

In this chapter, we have learned how to use the Facade pattern. This pattern is ideal for providing a simple interface to client code that wants to use a complex system but does not need to be aware of the system's complexity. A computer is a Facade, since all we need to use it is to press a single button for turning it on. All the rest hardware complexity is handled transparently by the BIOS, the boot loader, and the rest system software. There are more real-life examples of Facade, such as when we are connected to the customer service department of a bank, or a company, and the keys that we use to turn a vehicle on.

We discussed two Django third-party modules that use Facade: django-oscar-datacash and Caliendo. The first uses the Facade pattern to provide a simple DataCash API, and the ability to save transactions. The latter uses Facade for different purposes, like caching and deciding what should be returned based on the type of the input object.

We covered the basic use cases of Facade and ended the chapter with an implementation of the interface used by a multi-server operating system. A Facade is an elegant way of hiding the complexity of a system, because in most cases the client code should not be aware of such details.

In the next chapter, we will learn how to use the Flyweight design pattern for reusing objects to improve the resource usage of a system.

7
The Flyweight Pattern

Object-oriented systems can face performance issues due to the overhead of object creation. Performance issues usually appear in *embedded* systems with limited resources, such as smartphones and tablets. The same problem can appear in large and complex systems are where we need to create a very large number of objects (and possibly users) that need to coexist at the same time.

This happens because whenever we create a new object, extra memory needs to be allocated. Although virtual memory provides us, theoretically, with unlimited memory, the reality is different. If all the physical memory of a system gets exhausted, it will start swapping pages to the secondary storage, usually a **Hard Disk Drive (HDD)**, which, in most cases, is unacceptable due to the performance differences between the main memory and HDD. **Solid State Drives (SSD)** generally have better performance than HDD, but not everybody is expected to use SSD. So, SSD are not going to totally replace HDD anytime soon [j.mp/wissd].

Apart from memory usage, performance is also a consideration. Graphics software, including computer games, should be able to render 3D information (for example, a forest with thousands of trees or a village full of soldiers) extremely fast. If each object of a 3D terrain is created individually and no data sharing is used, the performance will be prohibitive [j.mp/flyweightp].

As software engineers, we should solve software problems by writing better software, instead of forcing the customer to buy extra or better hardware. The Flyweight design pattern is a technique used to minimize memory usage and improve performance by introducing data sharing between similar objects [j.mp/wflyw]. A **Flyweight** is a shared object that contains state-independent, immutable (also known as intrinsic) data. The state-dependent, mutable (also known as extrinsic) data should not be part of Flyweight because this is information that cannot be shared since it differs per object. If Flyweight needs extrinsic data, they should be provided explicitly by the client code [GOF95, page 219], [j.mp/smflywe].

An example might help to clarify how the Flyweight pattern can be practically used. Let's assume that we are creating a performance-critical game, for example, a **First-Person Shooter (FPS)**. In FPS games, the players (soldiers) share some states, such as representation and behavior. In Counter-Strike, for instance, all soldiers of the same team (counter-terrorists versus terrorists) look the same (representation). In the same game, all soldiers (of both teams) have some common actions, such as jump, duck, and so forth (behavior). This means that we can create a Flyweight that will contain all the common data. Of course, the soldiers also have many mutable data that are different per soldier and will not be a part of the Flyweight, such as weapons, health, locations, and so on.

A real-life example

Flyweight is an optimization design pattern; therefore, it is not easy to find a good real-life example of it. We can think of Flyweight as caching in real life. For example, many bookstores have dedicated shelves with the newest and most popular publications. This is a cache. First, you can take a look at the dedicated shelves for the book you are looking for, and if you cannot find it, you can ask the librarian to assist you.

A software example

The **Exaile** music player [j.mp/exaile] uses Flyweight to reuse objects (in this case, music tracks) that are identified by the same URL. There's no point in creating a new object if it has the same URL as an existing object, so the same object is reused to save resources [j.mp/exailefly].

Peppy, an XEmacs-like editor implemented in Python [j.mp/peppyp], uses the Flyweight pattern to store the state of a major mode status bar. That's because unless modified by the user, all status bars share the same properties [j.mp/peepyfly].

Use cases

Flyweight is all about improving performance and memory usage. All embedded systems (phones, tablets, game consoles, microcontrollers, and so forth) and performance-critical applications (games, 3D graphics processing, real-time systems, and so forth) can benefit from it.

The *Gang Of Four (GoF)* book lists the following requirements that need to be satisfied to effectively use the Flyweight Pattern [GOF95, page 221]:

- The application needs to use a large number of objects.

- There are so many objects that it's too expensive to store/render them. Once the mutable state is removed (because if it is required, it should be passed explicitly to Flyweight by the client code), many groups of distinct objects can be replaced by relatively few shared objects.

- Object identity is not important for the application. We cannot rely on object identity because object sharing causes identity comparisons to fail (objects that appear different to the client code, end up having the same identity).

Implementation

Since I already mentioned the tree example, let's see how we can implement it. In this example, we will create a very small forest of fruit trees. It is small to make sure that the whole output is readable in a single terminal page. However, no matter how large you make the forest, the memory allocation stays the same. An Enum parameter describes the three different types of fruit trees as follows:

```
TreeType = Enum('TreeType', 'apple_tree cherry_tree peach_tree')
```

Before diving into the code, let's spend a moment to note the difference between memoization and the Flyweight pattern. Memoization is an optimization technique that uses a cache to avoid recomputing results that were already computed in an earlier execution step. Memoization does not focus on a specific programming paradigm such as **object-oriented programming (OOP)**. In Python, memoization can be applied on both methods and simple functions. Flyweight is an OOP-specific optimization design pattern that focuses on sharing object data.

Flyweight can be implemented in Python in many ways, but I find the implementation shown in this example very neat. The pool variable is the object pool (in other words, our cache). Notice that pool is a class attribute (a variable shared by all instances) [j.mp/diveclsattr]. Using the __new__() special method, which is called before __init__(), we are converting the Tree class to a metaclass that supports self-references. This means that cls references the Tree class [Lott14, page 99]. When the client code creates an instance of Tree, they pass the type of the tree as tree_type. The type of the tree is used to check if a tree of the same type has already been created. If that's the case, the previously created object is returned; otherwise, the new tree type is added to the pool and returned as shown:

```
def __new__(cls, tree_type):
    obj = cls.pool.get(tree_type, None)
```

```
        if not obj:
            obj = object.__new__(cls)
            cls.pool[tree_type] = obj
            obj.tree_type = tree_type
    return obj
```

The `render()` method is what will be used to render a tree on the screen. Notice how all the mutable (extrinsic) information not known by Flyweight needs to be explicitly passed by the client code. In this case, a random age and a location of form *x, y* is used for every tree. To make `render()` more useful, it is necessary to ensure that no trees are rendered on top of each other. Consider this as an exercise. If you want to make rendering more fun, you can use a graphics toolkit such as Tkinter or Pygame.

```
def render(self, age, x, y):
        print('render a tree of type {} and age {} at ({},
        {})'.format(self.tree_type, age, x, y))
```

The `main()` function shows how we can use the Flyweight pattern. The age of a tree is a random value between 1 and 30 years. The coordinate uses random values between 1 and 100. Although eighteen trees are rendered, memory is allocated only for three. The last line of the output proves that when using Flyweight, we cannot rely on object identity. The `id()` function returns the memory address of an object. This is not the default behavior in Python because by default, `id()` returns a unique ID (actually the memory address of an object as an integer) for each object. In our case, even if two objects appear to be different, they actually have the same identity if they belong to the same Flyweight family (in this case, the family is defined by `tree_type`). Of course, different identity comparisons can still be used for objects of different families, but that is possible only if the client knows the implementation details (which is not the case usually).

```
def main():
    rnd = random.Random()
    age_min, age_max = 1, 30    # in years
    min_point, max_point = 0, 100
    tree_counter = 0

    for _ in range(10):
        t1 = Tree(TreeType.apple_tree)
        t1.render(rnd.randint(age_min, age_max),
                rnd.randint(min_point, max_point),
                rnd.randint(min_point, max_point))
        tree_counter += 1
```

```
        for _ in range(3):
            t2 = Tree(TreeType.cherry_tree)
            t2.render(rnd.randint(age_min, age_max),
                      rnd.randint(min_point, max_point),
                      rnd.randint(min_point, max_point))
            tree_counter += 1

        for _ in range(5):
            t3 = Tree(TreeType.peach_tree)
            t3.render(rnd.randint(age_min, age_max),
                      rnd.randint(min_point, max_point),
                      rnd.randint(min_point, max_point))
            tree_counter += 1

    print('trees rendered: {}'.format(tree_counter))
    print('trees actually created: {}'.format(len(Tree.pool)))

    t4 = Tree(TreeType.cherry_tree)
    t5 = Tree(TreeType.cherry_tree)
    t6 = Tree(TreeType.apple_tree)
    print('{} == {}? {}'.format(id(t4), id(t5), id(t4) == id(t5)))
    print('{} == {}? {}'.format(id(t5), id(t6), id(t5) == id(t6)))
```

The following full code listing (file flyweight.py) will give the complete picture of how the Flyweight pattern is implemented and used:

```
import random
from enum import Enum

TreeType = Enum('TreeType', 'apple_tree cherry_tree peach_tree')

class Tree:
    pool = dict()

    def __new__(cls, tree_type):
        obj = cls.pool.get(tree_type, None)
        if not obj:
            obj = object.__new__(cls)
            cls.pool[tree_type] = obj
            obj.tree_type = tree_type
        return obj
```

```python
    def render(self, age, x, y):
        print('render a tree of type {} and age {} at ({},
        {})'.format(self.tree_type, age, x, y))

def main():
    rnd = random.Random()
    age_min, age_max = 1, 30    # in years
    min_point, max_point = 0, 100
    tree_counter = 0

    for _ in range(10):
        t1 = Tree(TreeType.apple_tree)
        t1.render(rnd.randint(age_min, age_max),
                rnd.randint(min_point, max_point),
                rnd.randint(min_point, max_point))
        tree_counter += 1

    for _ in range(3):
        t2 = Tree(TreeType.cherry_tree)
        t2.render(rnd.randint(age_min, age_max),
                rnd.randint(min_point, max_point),
                rnd.randint(min_point, max_point))
        tree_counter += 1

    for _ in range(5):
        t3 = Tree(TreeType.peach_tree)
        t3.render(rnd.randint(age_min, age_max),
                rnd.randint(min_point, max_point),
                rnd.randint(min_point, max_point))
        tree_counter += 1

    print('trees rendered: {}'.format(tree_counter))
    print('trees actually created: {}'.format(len(Tree.pool)))

    t4 = Tree(TreeType.cherry_tree)
    t5 = Tree(TreeType.cherry_tree)
    t6 = Tree(TreeType.apple_tree)
    print('{} == {}? {}'.format(id(t4), id(t5), id(t4) == id(t5)))
    print('{} == {}? {}'.format(id(t5), id(t6), id(t5) == id(t6)))

if __name__ == '__main__':
    main()
```

The execution of the preceding example shows the type, random age, and coordinates of the rendered objects, as well as the identity comparison results between Flyweight objects of the same/different families. Do not expect to see the same output as the following since the ages and coordinates are random, and the object identities depend on the memory map.

```
>>> python3 flyweight.py
render a tree of type TreeType.apple_tree and age 4 at (88, 19)
render a tree of type TreeType.apple_tree and age 18 at (31, 35)
render a tree of type TreeType.apple_tree and age 7 at (54, 23)
render a tree of type TreeType.apple_tree and age 3 at (9, 11)
render a tree of type TreeType.apple_tree and age 2 at (93, 6)
render a tree of type TreeType.apple_tree and age 12 at (3, 49)
render a tree of type TreeType.apple_tree and age 10 at (5, 65)
render a tree of type TreeType.apple_tree and age 6 at (19, 16)
render a tree of type TreeType.apple_tree and age 2 at (21, 32)
render a tree of type TreeType.apple_tree and age 21 at (87, 79)
render a tree of type TreeType.cherry_tree and age 24 at (94, 31)
render a tree of type TreeType.cherry_tree and age 14 at (92, 37)
render a tree of type TreeType.cherry_tree and age 14 at (9, 88)
render a tree of type TreeType.peach_tree and age 23 at (44, 90)
render a tree of type TreeType.peach_tree and age 16 at (15, 59)
render a tree of type TreeType.peach_tree and age 1 at (81, 98)
render a tree of type TreeType.peach_tree and age 13 at (67, 63)
render a tree of type TreeType.peach_tree and age 12 at (69, 42)
trees rendered: 18
trees actually created: 3
140322427827480 == 140322427827480? True
140322427827480 == 140322427709088? False
```

Here's an exercise if you want to play more with Flyweight. Implement the FPS soldier example mentioned in this chapter. Think about which data should be part of Flyweight (immutable, intrinsic) and which should not (mutable, extrinsic).

Summary

In this chapter, we covered the Flyweight pattern. We can use Flyweight when we want to improve the memory usage and possibly the performance of our application. This is quite important in all systems with limited resources (think of embedded systems) and systems that focus on performance, such as graphics software and electronic games. The Exaile music player for GTK+ uses Flyweight to avoid object duplication, and the Peppy text editor uses it to share the properties of the status bar.

In general we use Flyweight when an application needs to create a large number of computationally expensive objects that share many properties. The important point is to separate the immutable (shared) properties, from the mutable. We implemented a tree renderer that supports three different tree families. By providing the mutable age and x, y properties explicitly to the `render()` method, we managed to create only three different objects instead of eighteen. Although that might not seem like a big win, imagine if the trees were two thousand instead of eighteen.

The next chapter covers a very popular design pattern that is used to keep the code that handles the user interface decoupled from the code that handles the (business) logic: Model-View-Controller.

8

The Model-View-Controller Pattern

One of the design principles related to software engineering is the **Separation of Concerns** (**SoC**) principle. The idea behind the SoC principle is to split an application into distinct sections, where each section addresses a separate concern. Examples of such concerns are the layers used in a layered design (data access layer, business logic layer, presentation layer, and so forth). Using the SoC principle simplifies the development and maintenance of software applications [j.mp/wikisoc].

The **Model-View-Controller** (**MVC**) pattern is nothing more than the SoC principle applied to OOP. The name of the pattern comes from the three main components used to split a software application: the model, the view, and the controller. MVC is considered an architectural pattern rather than a design pattern. The difference between an architectural and a design pattern is that the former has a broader scope than the latter. Nevertheless, MVC is too important to skip just for this reason. Even if we will never have to implement it from scratch, we need to be familiar with it because all common frameworks use MVC or a slightly different version of it (more on this later).

The model is the core component. It represents knowledge. It contains and manages the (business) logic, data, state, and rules of an application. The view is a visual representation of the model. Examples of views are a computer GUI, the text output of a computer terminal, a smartphone's application GUI, a PDF document, a pie chart, a bar chart, and so forth. The view only displays the data, it doesn't handle it. The controller is the link/glue between the model and view. All communication between the model and the view happens through a controller [GOF95, page 14], [j.mp/cohomvc], [j.mp/wikipmvc].

A typical use of an application that uses MVC after the initial screen is rendered to the user is as follows:

- The user triggers a view by clicking (typing, touching, and so on) a button
- The view informs the controller about the user's action
- The controller processes user input and interacts with the model
- The model performs all the necessary validation and state changes, and informs the controller about what should be done
- The controller instructs the view to update and display the output appropriately, following the instructions given by the model

You might be wondering why is the controller part necessary? Can't we just skip it? We could, but then we would lose a big benefit that MVC provides: the ability to use more than one view (even at the same time, if that's what we want) without modifying the model. To achieve decoupling between the model and its representation, every view typically needs its own controller. If the model communicated directly with a specific view, we wouldn't be able to use multiple views (or at least, not in a clean and modular way).

A real-life example

MVC is the SoC principle applied to OOP. The SoC principle is used a lot in real life. For example, if you build a new house, you usually assign different professionals to:

- Install the plumbing and electricity
- Paint the house

Another example is a restaurant. In a restaurant, the waiters receive orders and serve dishes to the customers, but the meals are cooked by the chefs [j.mp/somvc].

A software example

The **web2py** web framework [j.mp/webtopy] is a lightweight Python framework that embraces the MVC pattern. If you have never tried web2py, I encourage you to do it since it is extremely simple to install. All I had to do was download a package and execute a single Python file (web2py.py). There are many examples that demonstrate how MVC can be used in web2py on the project's web page [j.mp/web2pyex].

Django is also an MVC framework, although it uses different naming conventions. The controller is called view, and the view is called template. Django uses the name **Model-Template-View (MTV)**. According to the designers of Django, the view describes what data is seen by the user, and therefore, it uses the name view as the Python callback function for a particular URL. The term Template in Django is used to separate content from representation. It describes *how* the data is seen by the user, not *which* data is seen [j.mp/djangomtv].

Use cases

MVC is a very generic and useful design pattern. In fact, all popular Web frameworks (Django, Rails, and Yii) and application frameworks (iPhone SDK, Android, and QT) make use of MVC or a variation of it (**Model-View-Adapter (MVA)**, **Model-View-Presenter (MVP)**, and so forth). However, even if we don't use any of these frameworks, it makes sense to implement the pattern on our own because of the benefits it provides, which are as follows:

- The separation between the view and model allows graphics designers to focus on the UI part and programmers to focus on development, without interfering with each other.

- Because of the loose coupling between the view and model, each part can be modified/extended without affecting the other. For example, adding a new view is trivial. Just implement a new controller for it.

- Maintaining each part is easier because the responsibilities are clear.

When implementing MVC from scratch, be sure that you create smart models, thin controllers, and dumb views [Zlobin13, page 9].

A model is considered smart because it:

- Contains all the validation/business rules/logic
- Handles the state of the application
- Has access to application data (database, cloud, and so on)
- Does not depend on the UI

A controller is considered thin because it:

- Updates the model when the user interacts with the view
- Updates the view when the model changes
- Processes the data before delivering it to the model/view, if necessary

- Does not display the data
- Does not access the application data directly
- Does not contain validation/business rules/logic

A view is considered dumb because it:

- Displays the data
- Allows the user to interact with it
- Does only minimal processing, usually provided by a template language (for example, using simple variables and loop controls)
- Does not store any data
- Does not access the application data directly
- Does not contain validation/business rules/logic

If you are implementing MVC from scratch and want to find out if you did it right, you can try answering two key questions:

- If your application has a GUI, is it *skinnable*? How easily can you change the skin/look and feel of it? Can you give the user the ability to change the skin of your application during runtime? If this is not simple, it means that something is going wrong with your MVC implementation [j.mp/cohomvc].
- If your application has no GUI (for instance, if it's a terminal application), how hard is it to add GUI support? Or, if adding a GUI is irrelevant, is it easy to add views to display the results in a chart (pie chart, bar chart, and so on) or a document (PDF, spreadsheet, and so on)? If these changes are not trivial (a matter of creating a new controller with a view attached to it, without modifying the model), MVC is not implemented properly.

If you make sure that these two conditions are satisfied, your application will be more flexible and maintainable compared to an application that does not use MVC.

Implementation

I could use any of the common frameworks to demonstrate how to use MVC but I feel that the picture will be incomplete. So I decided to show how to implement MVC from scratch, using a very simple example: a quote printer. The idea is extremely simple. The user enters a number and sees the quote related to that number. The quotes are stored in a `quotes` tuple. This is the data that normally exists in a database, file, and so on, and only the model has direct access to it.

Let's consider the example in the following code:

```
quotes = ('A man is not complete until he is married. Then he is
          finished.', 'As I said before, I never repeat myself.',
          'Behind a successful man is an exhausted woman.',
          'Black holes really suck...', 'Facts are stubborn
          things.')
```

The model is minimalistic. It only has a get_quote() method that returns the quote (string) of the quotes tuple based on its index n. Note that n can be less than or equal to 0, due to the way indexing works in Python. Improving this behavior is given as an exercise for you at the end of this section.

```
class QuoteModel:
    def get_quote(self, n):
        try:
            value = quotes[n]
        except IndexError as err:
            value = 'Not found!'
        return value
```

The view has three methods: show(), which is used to print a quote (or the message **Not found!**) on the screen, error(), which is used to print an error message on the screen, and select_quote(), which reads the user's selection. This can be seen in the following code:

```
class QuoteTerminalView:
    def show(self, quote):
        print('And the quote is: "{}"'.format(quote))

    def error(self, msg):
        print('Error: {}'.format(msg))

    def select_quote(self):
        return input('Which quote number would you like to see? ')
```

The controller does the coordination. The __init__() method initializes the model and view. The run() method validates the quote index given by the user, gets the quote by the model, and passes it back to the view to be displayed as shown in the following code:

```
class QuoteTerminalController:
    def __init__(self):
        self.model = QuoteModel()
        self.view = QuoteTerminalView()
```

```
def run(self):
    valid_input = False
    while not valid_input:
        n = self.view.select_quote()
        try:
            n = int(n)
        except ValueError as err:
            self.view.error("Incorrect index '{}'".format(n))
        else:
            valid_input = True
    quote = self.model.get_quote(n)
    self.view.show(quote)
```

Last but not least, the `main()` function initializes and fires the controller as shown in the following code:

```
def main():
    controller = QuoteTerminalController()
    while True:
        controller.run()
```

The following is the full code of the example (file `mvc.py`):

```
quotes = ('A man is not complete until he is married. Then he is
          finished.', 'As I said before, I never repeat myself.',
          'Behind a successful man is an exhausted woman.',
          'Black holes really suck...', 'Facts are stubborn
          things.')

class QuoteModel:
    def get_quote(self, n):
        try:
            value = quotes[n]
        except IndexError as err:
            value = 'Not found!'
        return value

class QuoteTerminalView:
    def show(self, quote):
        print('And the quote is: "{}"'.format(quote))

    def error(self, msg):
        print('Error: {}'.format(msg))
```

```
        def select_quote(self):
            return input('Which quote number would you like to see? ')

    class QuoteTerminalController:
        def __init__(self):
            self.model = QuoteModel()
            self.view = QuoteTerminalView()

        def run(self):
            valid_input = False
            while not valid_input:
                try:
                    n = self.view.select_quote()
                    n = int(n)
                    valid_input = True
                except ValueError as err:
                    self.view.error("Incorrect index '{}'".format(n))
            quote = self.model.get_quote(n)
            self.view.show(quote)

    def main():
        controller = QuoteTerminalController()
        while True:
            controller.run()

    if __name__ == '__main__':
        main()
```

A sample execution of mvc.py shows how the program handles errors and prints quotes to the user:

```
>>> python3 mvc.py
Which quote number would you like to see? a
Error: Incorrect index 'a'
Which quote number would you like to see? 40
And the quote is: "Not found!"
Which quote number would you like to see? 0
And the quote is: "A man is not complete until he is married. Then he is
finished."
Which quote number would you like to see? 3
And the quote is: "Black holes really suck..."
```

Of course, you don't (and shouldn't) have to stop here. Keep coding. There are many interesting ideas that you can experiment with. A few of them are:

- Make the program more user-friendly by allowing only indexes of values greater than or equal to 1 to be given by the user. You will also need to modify `get_quote()`.

- Add a graphical view using a GUI framework such as Tkinter, Pygame, or Kivy. How modular is the program? Can you decide during runtime which view will be used?

- Give the user an option to view a random quote by typing a key, for example, key `r`.

- The index validation is currently done in the controller. Is that a good approach? What happens if you write another view that needs its own controller? Think about the changes required to move index validation in the model to make the code reusable for all controller/view pairs.

- Extend this example to make it work like a **Create, Read, Update, Delete (CRUD)** application. You should be able to enter new quotes, delete existing quotes, and modify a quote.

Summary

In this chapter, we covered the MVC pattern. MVC is a very important design pattern used to structure an application in three parts: the model, the view, and the controller.

Each part has clear roles and responsibilities. The model has access to the data and manages the state of the application. The view is a representation of the model. The view does not need to be graphical; textual output is also considered a totally fine view. The controller is the link between the model and view. Proper use of MVC guarantees that we end up with an application that is easy to maintain and extend.

The MVC pattern is the SoC principle applied to object-oriented programming. This principle is similar to how a new house is constructed or how a restaurant is operated.

The web2py Python framework uses MVC as the core architectural idea. Even the simplest web2py examples make use of MVC to achieve modularity and maintainability. Django is also an MVC framework, although it uses the name MTV.

When using MVC, make sure that you creating smart models (core functionality), thin controllers (functionality required for the communication between the view and the controller), and dumb views (representation and minimal processing).

In the *Implementation* section, we saw how to implement MVC from scratch to show funny quotes to the user. This is not very different from the functionality required to listing all the posts of an RSS feed. Feel free to implement this as an exercise, if none of the other recommended exercises appeal to you.

In the next chapter, you will learn how to secure an interface using an extra protection layer, implemented using the Proxy design pattern.

9

The Proxy Pattern

In some applications, we want to execute one or more important action before accessing an object. An example is accessing sensitive information. Before allowing any user to access sensitive information, we want to make sure that the user has sufficient privileges. A similar situation exists in operating systems. A user is required to have administrative privileges to install new programs system-wide.

The important action is not necessarily related to security issues. Lazy initialization [j.mp/wikilazy] is another case; we want to delay the creation of a computationally expensive object until the first time the user actually needs to use it.

Such actions are typically performed using the **Proxy design pattern**. The pattern gets its name from the proxy (also known as surrogate) object used to perform an important action before accessing the actual object. There are four different well-known proxy types [GOF95, page 234], [j.mp/proxypat]. They are as follows:

- A **remote proxy**, which acts as the local representation of an object that really exists in a different address space (for example, a network server).

- A **virtual proxy**, which uses lazy initialization to defer the creation of a computationally expensive object until the moment it is actually needed.

- A **protection/protective proxy**, which controls access to a sensitive object.

- A **smart (reference) proxy**, which performs extra actions when an object is accessed. Examples of such actions are reference counting and thread-safety checks.

I find virtual proxies very useful so let's see an example of how we can implement them in Python right now. In the *Implementation* section, you will learn how to create protective proxies.

There are many ways to create a virtual proxy in Python, but I always like focusing on the idiomatic/pythonic implementations. The code shown here is based on the great answer by Cyclone, a user of the site `stackoverflow.com` [j.mp/solazyinit]. To avoid confusion, I should clarify that in this section, the terms property, variable, and attribute are used interchangeably. First, we create a `LazyProperty` class that can be used as a decorator. When it decorates a property, `LazyProperty` loads the property lazily (on the first use) instead of instantly. The `__init__()` method creates two variables that are used as aliases to the method that initializes a property. The `method` variable is an alias to the actual method, and the `method_name` variable is an alias to the method's name. To get a better understanding about how the two aliases are used, print their value to the output (uncomment the two commented lines in the following code):

```
class LazyProperty:
    def __init__(self, method):
        self.method = method
        self.method_name = method.__name__
        # print('function overriden: {}'.format(self.fget))
        # print("function's name: {}".format(self.func_name))
```

The `LazyProperty` class is actually a descriptor [j.mp/pydesc]. **Descriptors** are the recommended mechanism to use in Python to override the default behavior of its attribute access methods: `__get__()`, `__set__()`, and `__delete__()`. The `LazyProperty` class overrides only `__set__()` because that is the only access method it needs to override. In other words, we don't have to override all access methods. The `__get__()` method accesses the value of the property the underlying method wants to assign, and uses `setattr()` to do the assignment manually. What `__get()__` actually does is very neat; it replaces the method with the value! This means that not only is the property lazily loaded, it can also be set only once. We will see what this means in a moment. Again, uncomment the commented line in the following code to get some extra info:

```
    def __get__(self, obj, cls):
        if not obj:
            return None
        value = self.method(obj)
        # print('value {}'.format(value))
        setattr(obj, self.method_name, value)
        return value
```

The Test class shows how we can use the LazyProperty class. There are three attributes: x, y, and _resource. We want the _resource variable to be loaded lazily; thus, we initialize it to None as shown in the following code:

```
class Test:
    def __init__(self):
        self.x = 'foo'
        self.y = 'bar'
        self._resource = None
```

The resource() method is decorated with the LazyProperty class. For demonstration purposes, the LazyProperty class initializes the _resource attribute as a tuple as shown in the following code. Normally, this would be a slow/expensive initialization (database, graphics, and so on):

```
@LazyProperty
def resource(self):
    print('initializing self._resource which is:
    {}'.format(self._resource))
    self._resource = tuple(range(5)) # expensive
    return self._resource
```

The main() function shows how lazy initialization behaves. Notice how overriding the __get__() access method makes it possible to treat the resource() method as a variable (we can use t.resource instead of t.resource()):

```
def main():
    t = Test()
    print(t.x)
    print(t.y)
    # do more work...
    print(t.resource)
    print(t.resource)
```

In the execution output of this example (the lazy.py file), we can see that:

- The _resource variable is indeed initialized not by the time the t instance is created, but the first time that we use t.resource.

- The second time t.resource is used, the variable is not initialized again. That's why the initialization string **initializing self._resource which is:** is shown only once.

- The following shows the execution of the `lazy.py` file:

```
>>> python3 lazy.py
foo
bar
initializing self._resource which is: None
(0, 1, 2, 3, 4)
(0, 1, 2, 3, 4)
```

There are two basic, different kinds of lazy initialization in OOP. They are as follows:

- **At the instance level**: This means that an object's property is initialized lazily, but the property has an object scope. Each instance (object) of the same class has its own (different) copy of the property.

- **At the class or module level**: In this case, we do not want a different copy per instance, but all the instances share the same property, which is lazily initialized. This case is not covered in this chapter. If you find it interesting, consider it as an exercise.

A real-life example

Chip (also known as Chip and PIN) cards [j.mp/wichpin] are a good example of a protective proxy used in real life. The debit/credit card contains a chip that first needs to be read by the ATM or card reader. After the chip is verified, a password (PIN) is required to complete the transaction. This means that you cannot make any transactions without physically presenting the card and knowing the PIN.

A bank check that is used instead of cash to make purchases and deals is an example of a remote proxy. The check gives access to a bank account. The following figure, courtesy of `sourcemaking.com`, shows how a check acts as a remote proxy [j.mp/proxypat]:

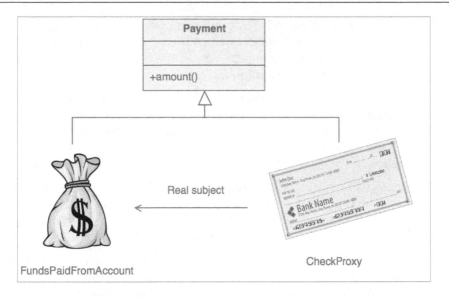

A software example

The weakref module of Python contains a proxy() method that accepts an input object and returns a smart proxy to it. Weak references are the recommended way to add a reference counting support to an object [j.mp/wrefproxy].

ZeroMQ [j.mp/zermq] is a set of FOSS projects that focus on decentralized computing. The Python implementation of ZeroMQ has a proxy module that implements a remote proxy. This module allows Tornado [j.mp/pytornado] handlers to be run in separate remote processes [j.mp/pyzmq].

Use cases

Since there are at least four common proxy types, the Proxy design pattern has many use cases, as follows:

- It is used when creating a distributed system using either a private network or the cloud. In a distributed system, some objects exist in the local memory and some objects exist in the memory of remote computers. If we don't want the client code to be aware of such differences, we can create a remote proxy that hides/encapsulates them, making the distributed nature of the application transparent.

- It is used if our application is suffering from performance issues due to the early creation of expensive objects. Introducing lazy initialization using a virtual proxy to create the objects only at the moment they are actually required can give us significant performance improvements.

- It is used to check if a user has sufficient privileges to access a piece of information. If our application handles sensitive information (for example, medical data), we want to make sure that the user trying to access/modify it is allowed to do so. A protection/protective proxy can handle all security-related actions.

- It is used when our application (or library, toolkit, framework, and so forth) uses multiple threads and we want to move the burden of thread-safety from the client code to the application. In this case, we can create a smart proxy to hide the thread-safety complexities from the client.

- An **Object-Relational Mapping (ORM)** API is also an example of how to use a remote proxy. Many popular web frameworks, including Django, use an ORM to provide OOP-like access to a relational database. An ORM acts as a proxy to a relational database that can be actually located anywhere, either at a local or remote server.

Implementation

To demonstrate the Proxy pattern, we will implement a simple protection proxy to view and add users. The service provides two options:

- **Viewing the list of users**: This operation does not require special privileges

- **Adding a new user**: This operation requires the client to provide a special secret message

The `SensitiveInfo` class contains the information that we want to protect. The `users` variable is the list of existing users. The `read()` method prints the list of the users. The `add()` method adds a new user to the list. Let's consider the following code:

```
class SensitiveInfo:
    def __init__(self):
        self.users = ['nick', 'tom', 'ben', 'mike']

    def read(self):
        print('There are {} users: {}'.format(len(self.users), '
        '.join(self.users)))

    def add(self, user):
        self.users.append(user)
        print('Added user {}'.format(user))
```

The `Info` class is a protection proxy of `SensitiveInfo`. The `secret` variable is the message required to be known/provided by the client code to add a new user. Note that this is just an example. In reality, you should *never*:

- Store passwords in the source code
- Store passwords in a clear-text form
- Use a weak (for example, MD5) or custom form of encryption

The `read()` method is a wrapper to `SensitiveInfo.read()`. The `add()` method ensures that a new user can be added only if the client code knows the secret message. Let's consider the following code:

```
class Info:
    def __init__(self):
        self.protected = SensitiveInfo()
        self.secret = '0xdeadbeef'

    def read(self):
        self.protected.read()

    def add(self, user):
        sec = input('what is the secret? ')
        self.protected.add(user) if sec == self.secret else
        print("That's wrong!")
```

The `main()` function shows how the Proxy pattern can be used by the client code. The client code creates an instance of the `Info` class and uses the displayed menu to read the list, add a new user, or exit the application. Let's consider the following code:

```
def main():
    info = Info()

    while True:
        print('1. read list |==| 2. add user |==| 3. quit')
        key = input('choose option: ')
        if key == '1':
            info.read()
        elif key == '2':
            name = input('choose username: ')
            info.add(name)
        elif key == '3':
            exit()
        else:
            print('unknown option: {}'.format(key))
```

Let's see the the full code of the `proxy.py` file:

```python
class SensitiveInfo:
    def __init__(self):
        self.users = ['nick', 'tom', 'ben', 'mike']

    def read(self):
        print('There are {} users: {}'.format(len(self.users), '
        '.join(self.users)))

    def add(self, user):
        self.users.append(user)
        print('Added user {}'.format(user))

class Info:
    '''protection proxy to SensitiveInfo'''

    def __init__(self):
        self.protected = SensitiveInfo()
        self.secret = '0xdeadbeef'

    def read(self):
        self.protected.read()

    def add(self, user):
        sec = input('what is the secret? ')
        self.protected.add(user) if sec == self.secret else
        print("That's wrong!")

def main():
    info = Info()

    while True:
        print('1. read list |==| 2. add user |==| 3. quit')
        key = input('choose option: ')
        if key == '1':
            info.read()
        elif key == '2':
            name = input('choose username: ')
            info.add(name)
        elif key == '3':
            exit()
        else:
            print('unknown option: {}'.format(key))

if __name__ == '__main__':
    main()
```

Here is an example of how to execute `proxy.py`:

```
>>> python3 proxy.py
1. read list |==| 2. add user |==| 3. quit
choose option: a
1. read list |==| 2. add user |==| 3. quit
choose option: 4
1. read list |==| 2. add user |==| 3. quit
choose option: 1
There are 4 users: nick tom ben mike
1. read list |==| 2. add user |==| 3. quit
choose option: 2
choose username: pet
what is the secret? blah
That's wrong!
1. read list |==| 2. add user |==| 3. quit
choose option: 2
choose username: bill
what is the secret? 0xdeadbeef
Added user bill
1. read list |==| 2. add user |==| 3. quit
choose option: 1
There are 5 users: nick tom ben mike bill
1. read list |==| 2. add user |==| 3. quit
choose option: 3
```

Have you already spotted flaws or missing features that can improve the Proxy example? I have a few suggestions. They are as follows:

- This example has a very big security flaw. Nothing prevents the client code from bypassing the security of the application by creating an instance of `SensitiveInfo` directly. Improve the example to prevent this situation. One way is to use the `abc` module to forbid direct instantiation of `SensitiveInfo`. What other code changes are required in this case?

- A basic security rule is that we should never store clear-text passwords. Storing a password safely is not very hard as long as we know which libraries to use [j.mp/hashsec]. If you have an interest in security, read the article and try to implement a secure way to store the secret message externally (for example, in a file or database).

- The application only supports adding new users, but what about removing an existing user? Add a `remove()` method. Should `remove()` be a privileged operation?

Summary

In this chapter, you learned how to use the Proxy design pattern. We used the Proxy pattern to implement a surrogate of an actual class when we want to act before (or after) accessing it. There are four different Proxy types. They are as follows:

- A remote proxy, which represents an object that lives in a remote location (for example, our own remote server or cloud service)

- A virtual proxy to delay the initialization of an object until it is actually used

- A protection/protective proxy, which is used to access control to an object that handles sensitive information

- When we want to extend the behavior of an object by adding support such as reference counting, we use a smart (reference) proxy

In the first code example, we created a virtual proxy in a pythonic style, using decorators and descriptors. This proxy allows us to initialize object properties in a lazy manner.

Chip and PIN and bank checks are examples of two different proxies used by people every day. Chip and PIN is a protective proxy, while a bank check is a remote proxy. However, proxies are also used in popular software. Python has a `weakref.proxy()` method that makes the creation of a smart proxy of an object very easy. The Python implementation of ZeroMQ uses a remote proxy.

We discussed several use cases of the Proxy pattern, including performance, security, and offering simple APIs to users. In the second code example, we implemented a protection proxy to handle users. This example can be improved in many ways, especially regarding its security flaws and the fact that the list of users is not persistent (permanently stored). Hopefully, you will find the recommended exercises interesting.

In the next chapter, we will explore behavioral design patterns. Behavioral patterns cope with object interconnection and algorithms. The first behavioral pattern that will be covered is Chain of Responsibility, which allows us to create a chain of receiving objects so that we can send broadcast messages. Sending a broadcast message is useful when the handler of a request is not known in advance.

10
The Chain of Responsibility Pattern

When developing an application, most of the time we know which method should satisfy a particular request in advance. However, this is not always the case. For example, we can think of any broadcast computer network, such as the original Ethernet implementation [j.mp/wikishared]. In broadcast computer networks, all requests are sent to all nodes (broadcast domains are excluded for simplicity), but only the nodes that are interested in a sent request process it. All computers that participate in a broadcast network are connected to each other using a common medium such as the cable that connects the three nodes in the following figure:

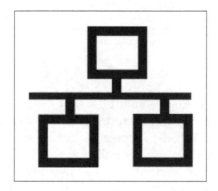

If a node is not interested or does not know how to handle a request, it can perform the following actions:

* Ignore the request and do nothing
* Forward the request to the next node

The way in which the node reacts to a request is an implementation detail. However, we can use the analogy of a broadcast computer network to understand what the chain of responsibility pattern is all about. The **Chain of Responsibility** pattern is used when we want to give a chance to multiple objects to satisfy a single request, or when we don't know which object (from a chain of objects) should process a specific request in advance. The principle is the same as the following:

1. There is a chain (linked list, tree, or any other convenient data structure) of objects.
2. We start by sending a request to the first object in the chain.
3. The object decides whether it should satisfy the request or not.
4. The object forwards the request to the next object.
5. This procedure is repeated until we reach the end of the chain.

At the application level, instead of talking about cables and network nodes, we can focus on objects and the flow of a request. The following figure, courtesy of www.sourcemaking.com [j.mp/smchain], shows how the client code sends a request to all processing elements (also known as nodes or handlers) of an application:

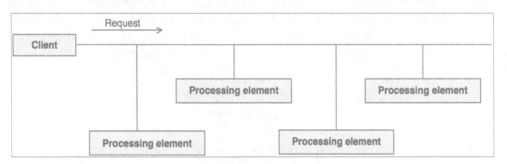

Note that the client code only knows about the first processing element, instead of having references to all of them, and each processing element only knows about its immediate next neighbor (called the successor), not about every other processing element. This is usually a one-way relationship, which in programming terms means a singly linked list in contrast to a doubly linked list; a singly linked list does not allow navigation in both ways, while a doubly linked list allows that. This chain organization is used for a good reason. It achieves decoupling between the sender (client) and the receivers (processing elements) [GOF95, page 254].

A real-life example

ATMs and, in general, any kind of machine that accepts/returns banknotes or coins (for example, a snack vending machine) use the chain of responsibility pattern. There is always a single slot for all banknotes, as shown in the following figure, courtesy of www.sourcemaking.com:

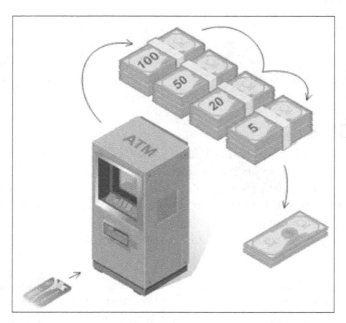

When a banknote is dropped, it is routed to the appropriate receptacle. When it is returned, it is taken from the appropriate receptacle [j.mp/smchain], [j.mp/c2chain]. We can think of the single slot as the shared communication medium and the different receptacles as the processing elements. The result contains cash from one or more receptacles. For example, in the preceding figure, we see what happens when we request $175 from the ATM.

A software example

I tried to find some good examples of Python applications that use the Chain of Responsibility pattern but I couldn't, most likely because Python programmers don't use this name. So, my apologies, but I will use other programming languages as a reference.

The servlet filters of Java are pieces of code that are executed before an HTTP request arrives at a target. When using servlet filters, there is a chain of filters. Each filter performs a different action (user authentication, logging, data compression, and so forth), and either forwards the request to the next filter until the chain is exhausted, or it breaks the flow if there is an error (for example, the authentication failed three consecutive times) [j.mp/soservl].

Apple's Cocoa and Cocoa Touch frameworks use Chain of Responsibility to handle events. When a view receives an event that it doesn't know how to handle, it forwards the event to its superview. This goes on until a view is capable of handling the event or the chain of views is exhausted [j.mp/chaincocoa].

Use cases

By using the Chain of Responsibility pattern, we give a chance to a number of different objects to satisfy a specific request. This is useful when we don't know which object should satisfy a request in advance. An example is a purchase system. In purchase systems, there are many approval authorities. One approval authority might be able to approve orders up to a certain value, let's say $100. If the order is more than $100, the order is sent to the next approval authority in the chain that can approve orders up to $200, and so forth.

Another case where Chain of Responsibility is useful is when we know that more than one object might need to process a single request. This is what happens in an event-based programming. A single event such as a left mouse click can be caught by more than one listener.

It is important to note that the Chain of Responsibility pattern is not very useful if all the requests can be taken care of by a single processing element, unless we really don't know which element that is. The value of this pattern is the decoupling that it offers. Instead of having a many-to-many relationship between a client and all processing elements (and the same is true regarding the relationship between a processing element and all other processing elements), a client only needs to know how to communicate with the start (head) of the chain.

The following figure demonstrates the difference between tight and loose coupling. The idea behind loosely coupled systems is to simplify maintenance and make it easier for us to understand how they function [j.mp/loosecoup]:

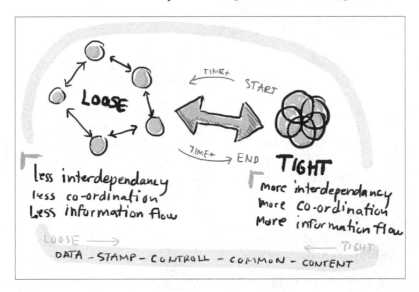

Implementation

There are many ways to implement Chain of Responsibility in Python, but my favorite implementation is the one by Vespe Savikko [j.mp/savviko]. Vespe's implementation uses dynamic dispatching in a Pythonic style to handle requests [j.mp/ddispatch].

Let's implement a simple event-based system using Vespe's implementation as a guide. The following is the UML class diagram of the system:

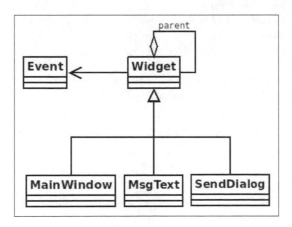

The Event class describes an event. We'll keep it simple, so in our case an event has only name:

```
class Event:
    def __init__(self, name):
        self.name = name

    def __str__(self):
        return self.name
```

The Widget class is the core class of the application. The parent aggregation shown in the UML diagram indicates that each widget can have a reference to a parent object, which by convention, we assume is a Widget instance. Note, however, that according to the rules of inheritance, an instance of any of the subclasses of Widget (for example, an instance of MsgText) is also an instance of Widget. The default value of parent is None:

```
class Widget:
    def __init__(self, parent=None):
        self.parent = parent
```

The handle() method uses dynamic dispatching through hasattr() and getattr() to decide who is the handler of a specific request (event). If the widget that is asked to handle an event does not support it, there are two fallback mechanisms. If the widget has parent, then the handle() method of parent is executed. If the widget has no parent but a handle_default() method, handle_default() is executed:

```
def handle(self, event):
    handler = 'handle_{}'.format(event)
    if hasattr(self, handler):
        method = getattr(self, handler)
        method(event)
    elif self.parent:
        self.parent.handle(event)
    elif hasattr(self, 'handle_default'):
        self.handle_default(event)
```

At this point, you might have realized why the Widget and Event classes are only associated (no aggregation or composition relationships) in the UML class diagram. The association is used to show that the Widget class "knows" about the Event class but does not have any strict references to it, since an event needs to be passed only as a parameter to handle().

MainWIndow, MsgText, and SendDialog are all widgets with different behaviors. Not all these three widgets are expected to be able to handle the same events, and even if they can handle the same event, they might behave differently. MainWIndow can handle only the close and default events:

```
class MainWindow(Widget):
    def handle_close(self, event):
        print('MainWindow: {}'.format(event))

    def handle_default(self, event):
        print('MainWindow Default: {}'.format(event))
```

SendDialog can handle only the paint event:

```
class SendDialog(Widget):
    def handle_paint(self, event):
        print('SendDialog: {}'.format(event))
```

Finally, MsgText can handle only the down event:

```
class MsgText(Widget):
    def handle_down(self, event):
        print('MsgText: {}'.format(event))
```

The main() function shows how we can create a few widgets and events, and how the widgets react to those events. All events are sent to all the widgets. Note the parent relationship of each widget. The sd object (an instance of SendDialog) has as its parent the mw object (an instance of MainWindow). However, not all objects need to have a parent that is an instance of MainWindow. For example, the msg object (an instance of MsgText) has the sd object as a parent:

```
def main():
    mw = MainWindow()
    sd = SendDialog(mw)
    msg = MsgText(sd)

    for e in ('down', 'paint', 'unhandled', 'close'):
        evt = Event(e)
        print('\nSending event -{}- to MainWindow'.format(evt))
        mw.handle(evt)
        print('Sending event -{}- to SendDialog'.format(evt))
        sd.handle(evt)
        print('Sending event -{}- to MsgText'.format(evt))
        msg.handle(evt)
```

The following is the full code of the example (`chain.py`):

```python
class Event:
    def __init__(self, name):
        self.name = name

    def __str__(self):
        return self.name

class Widget:
    def __init__(self, parent=None):
        self.parent = parent

    def handle(self, event):
        handler = 'handle_{}'.format(event)
        if hasattr(self, handler):
            method = getattr(self, handler)
            method(event)
        elif self.parent:
            self.parent.handle(event)
        elif hasattr(self, 'handle_default'):
            self.handle_default(event)

class MainWindow(Widget):
    def handle_close(self, event):
        print('MainWindow: {}'.format(event))

    def handle_default(self, event):
        print('MainWindow Default: {}'.format(event))

class SendDialog(Widget):
    def handle_paint(self, event):
        print('SendDialog: {}'.format(event))

class MsgText(Widget):
    def handle_down(self, event):
        print('MsgText: {}'.format(event))

def main():
    mw = MainWindow()
    sd = SendDialog(mw)
    msg = MsgText(sd)
```

```
for e in ('down', 'paint', 'unhandled', 'close'):
    evt = Event(e)
    print('\nSending event -{}- to MainWindow'.format(evt))
    mw.handle(evt)
    print('Sending event -{}- to SendDialog'.format(evt))
    sd.handle(evt)
    print('Sending event -{}- to MsgText'.format(evt))
    msg.handle(evt)

if __name__ == '__main__':
    main()
```

Executing chain.py gives us the following results:

```
>>> python3 chain.py


Sending event -down- to MainWindow
MainWindow Default: down
Sending event -down- to SendDialog
MainWindow Default: down
Sending event -down- to MsgText
MsgText: down

Sending event -paint- to MainWindow
MainWindow Default: paint
Sending event -paint- to SendDialog
SendDialog: paint
Sending event -paint- to MsgText
SendDialog: paint

Sending event -unhandled- to MainWindow
MainWindow Default: unhandled
Sending event -unhandled- to SendDialog
MainWindow Default: unhandled
Sending event -unhandled- to MsgText
MainWindow Default: unhandled
```

```
Sending event -close- to MainWindow
MainWindow: close
Sending event -close- to SendDialog
MainWindow: close
Sending event -close- to MsgText
MainWindow: close
```

There are some interesting things that we can see in the output. For instance, sending a `down` event to `MainWindow` ends up being handled by the default `MainWindow` handler. Another nice case is that although a `close` event cannot be handled directly by `SendDialog` and `MsgText`, all the close events end up being handled properly by `MainWindow`. That's the beauty of using the parent relationship as a fallback mechanism.

If you want to spend some more creative time on the event example, you can replace the dumb `print` statements and add some actual behavior to the listed events. Of course, you are not limited to the listed events. Just add your favorite event and make it do something useful!

Another exercise is to add a `MsgText` instance during runtime that has `MainWindow` as the parent. Is this hard? Do the same for an event (add a new event to an existing widget). Which is harder?

Summary

In this chapter, we covered the Chain of Responsibility design pattern. This pattern is useful to model requests / handle events when the number and type of handlers isn't known in advance. Examples of systems that fit well with Chain of Responsibility are event-based systems, purchase systems, and shipping systems.

In the Chain Of Responsibility pattern, the sender has direct access to the first node of a chain. If the request cannot be satisfied by the first node, it forwards to the next node. This continues until either the request is satisfied by a node or the whole chain is traversed. This design is used to achieve loose coupling between the sender and the receiver(s).

ATMs are an example of Chain Of Responsibility. The single slot that is used for all banknotes can be considered the head of the chain. From here, depending on the transaction, one or more receptacles is used to process the transaction. The receptacles can be considered the processing elements of the chain.

Java's servlet filters use the Chain of Responsibility pattern to perform different actions (for example, compression and authentication) on an HTTP request. Apple's Cocoa frameworks use the same pattern to handle events such as button presses and finger gestures.

The implementation section demonstrates how we can create our own event-based system in Python using dynamic dispatching.

The next chapter is about the Command pattern, which is used (but not limited to) to add undo support in an application.

11
The Command Pattern

Most applications nowadays have an undo operation. It is hard to imagine, but undo did not exist in any software for many years. Undo was introduced in 1974 [j.mp/wiundo], but Fortran and Lisp, two programming languages that are still widely used, were created in 1957 and 1958, respectively [j.mp/proghist]! I wouldn't like to be an application user during those years. Making a mistake meant that the user had no easy way to fix it.

Enough with the history. We want to know how we can implement the undo functionality in our applications. And since you have read the title of this chapter, you already know which design pattern is recommended to implement undo: **the Command pattern**.

The Command design pattern helps us encapsulate an operation (undo, redo, copy, paste, and so forth) as an object. What this simply means is that we create a class that contains all the logic and the methods required to implement the operation. The advantages of doing this are as follows [GOF95, page 265], [j.mp/cmdpattern]:

- We don't have to execute a command directly. It can be executed on will.

- The object that invokes the command is decoupled from the object that knows how to perform it. The invoker does not need to know any implementation details about the command.

- If it makes sense, multiple commands can be grouped to allow the invoker to execute them in order. This is useful, for instance, when implementing a multilevel undo command.

A real-life example

When we go to the restaurant for dinner, we give the order to the waiter. The check (usually paper) they use to write the order on is an example of Command. After writing the order, the waiter places it in the check queue that is executed by the cook. Each check is independent and can be used to execute many and different commands, for example, one command for each item that will be cooked. The following figure, courtesy of www.sourcemaking.com [j.mp/cmdpattern], shows a sequence diagram of a sample order:

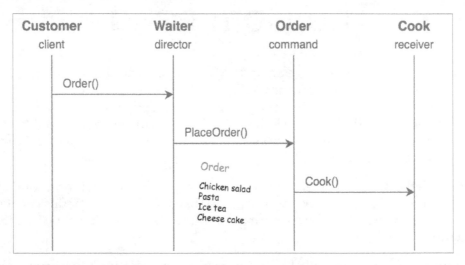

A software example

PyQt is the Python binding of the QT toolkit. PyQt contains a QAction class that models an action as a command. Extra optional information is supported for every action, such as description, tooltip, shortcut, and more [j.mp/qaction].

git-cola [j.mp/git-cola], a Git GUI written in Python, uses the Command pattern to modify the model, amend a commit, apply a different election, check out, and so forth [j.mp/git-cola-code].

Use cases

Many developers use the undo example as the only use case of the Command pattern. The truth is that undo is the killer feature of the Command pattern. However, the Command pattern can actually do much more [GOF95, page 265], [j.mp/commddp]:

- **GUI buttons and menu items**: The PyQt example that was already mentioned uses the Command pattern to implement actions on buttons and menu items.

- **Other operations**: Apart from undo, Command can be used to implement any operation. A few examples are cut, copy, paste, redo, and capitalize text.

- **Transactional behavior and logging**: Transactional behavior and logging are important to keep a persistent log of changes. They are used by operating systems to recover from system crashes, relational databases to implement transactions, filesystems to implement snapshots, and installers (wizards) to revert cancelled installations.

- **Macros**: By macros, in this case, we mean a sequence of actions that can be recorded and executed on demand at any point in time. Popular editors such as Emacs and Vim support macros.

Implementation

In this section, we will use the Command pattern to implement the most basic file utilities:

- Creating a file and optionally writing a string in it
- Reading the contents of a file
- Renaming a file
- Deleting a file

We will not implement these utilities from scratch, since Python already offers good implementations of them in the os module. What we want is to add an extra abstraction level on top of them so that they can be treated as commands. By doing this, we get all the advantages offered by commands.

The following use case diagram shows the supported operations that a user can execute. From the operations shown, renaming a file and creating a file support undo. Deleting a file and reading the contents of a file do no support undo. Undo can actually be implemented on delete file operations. One technique is to use a special trash/wastebasket directory that stores all the deleted files, so that they can be restored when the user requests it. This is the default behavior used on all modern desktop environments and is left as an exercise.

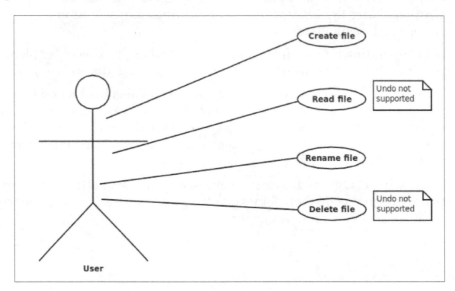

Each command has two parts: the initialization part and the execution part. The initialization part is taken care of by the __init__() method and contains all the information required by the command to be able to do something useful (the path of a file, the contents that will be written to the file, and so forth). The execution part is taken care by the execute() method. We call the execute() method when we want to actually run a command. This is not necessarily right after initializing it.

Let's start with the rename utility, which is implemented using the RenameFile class. The __init__() method accepts the source (path_src) and destination (path_dest) file paths as parameters (strings). If no path separators are used, the current directory is used to create the file. An example of using a path separator is passing the string /tmp/file1 as path_src and the string /home/user/file2 as path_dest. The example of not using a path is passing file1 as path_src and file2 as path_dest:

```
class RenameFile:
    def __init__(self, path_src, path_dest):
        self.src, self.dest = path_src, path_dest
```

The `execute()` method does the actual renaming using `os.rename()`. `verbose` is a global flag, which, when activated (by default, it is activated), gives feedback to the user about the operation that is performed. You can deactivate it if you prefer silent commands. Note that although `print()` is good enough for an example, normally something more mature and powerful can be used, for example, the logging module [`j.mp/py3log`]:

```
def execute(self):
    if verbose:
        print("[renaming '{}' to '{}']".format(self.src, self.
dest))
    os.rename(self.src, self.dest)
```

Our rename utility supports the undo operation through its `undo()` method. In this case, undo uses `os.rename()` again to revert the name of the file to its original value:

```
def undo(self):
    if verbose:
        print("[renaming '{}' back to '{}']".format(self.dest,
self.src))
    os.rename(self.dest, self.src)
```

Deleting a file is a single function, instead of a class. I did that to show you that it is not mandatory to create a new class for every command that you want to add (more on that will be covered later). The `delete_file()` function accepts a file path as a string and uses `os.remove()` to delete it:

```
def delete_file(path):
    if verbose:
        print("deleting file '{}".format(path))
    os.remove(path)
```

Back to using classes again. The `CreateFile` class is used to create a file. The `__init__()` function accepts the familiar `path` parameter and a `txt` string, which is the content that will be written to the file. If nothing is passed as `txt`, the default "hello world" text is written to the file. Normally, the sane default behavior is to create an empty file, but for the needs of this example, I decided to write a default string in it. Feel free to change it:

```
def __init__(self, path, txt='hello world\n'):
    self.path, self.txt = path, txt
```

The `execute()` method uses the `with` statement and `open()` to open the file (`mode='w'` means write mode), and `write()` to write the `txt` string:

```python
def execute(self):
    if verbose:
        print("[creating file '{}']".format(self.path))
    with open(self.path, mode='w', encoding='utf-8') as out_file:
        out_file.write(self.txt)
```

The undo operation of creating a file is to delete it. So, `undo()` simply uses `delete_file()` to achieve that:

```python
def undo(self):
    delete_file(self.path)
```

The last utility gives us the ability to read the contents of a file. The `execute()` method of the `ReadFile` class uses the `with` statement with `open()` again, this time in read mode, and just prints the contents of it using `print()`:

```python
def execute(self):
    if verbose:
        print("[reading file '{}']".format(self.path))
    with open(self.path, mode='r', encoding='utf-8') as in_file:
        print(in_file.read(), end='')
```

The `main()` function makes use of the utilities. The `orig_name` and `new_name` parameters are the original and new name of the file that is created and renamed. A `commands` list is used to add (and configure) all the commands that we want to execute at a later point. Note that the commands are not executed unless we explicitly call `execute()` for each command:

```python
orig_name, new_name = 'file1', 'file2'

commands = []
for cmd in CreateFile(orig_name), ReadFile(orig_name),
                RenameFile(orig_name, new_name):
    commands.append(cmd)

[c.execute() for c in commands]
```

The next step is to ask the users if they want to undo the executed commands or not. The user selects whether the commands will be undone or not. If they choose to undo them, undo() is executed for all commands in the commands list. However, since not all commands support undo, exception handling is used to catch (and ignore) the AttributeError exception generated when the undo() method is missing. If you don't like using exception handling for such cases, you can check explicitly whether a command supports the undo operation by adding a Boolean method, for example, supports_undo() or can_de_undone():

```
answer = input('reverse the executed commands? [y/n] ')



if answer not in 'yY':
    print("the result is {}".format(new_name))
    exit()

for c in reversed(commands):
    try:
        c.undo()
    except AttributeError as e:
        pass
```

Here's the full code of the example (command.py):

```python
import os

verbose = True

class RenameFile:
    def __init__(self, path_src, path_dest):
        self.src, self.dest = path_src, path_dest

    def execute(self):
        if verbose:
            print("[renaming '{}' to '{}']".format(self.src, self.
dest))
        os.rename(self.src, self.dest)

    def undo(self):
        if verbose:
            print("[renaming '{}' back to '{}']".format(self.dest,
self.src))
        os.rename(self.dest, self.src)
```

```python
class CreateFile:
    def __init__(self, path, txt='hello world\n'):
        self.path, self.txt = path, txt

    def execute(self):
        if verbose:
            print("[creating file '{}']".format(self.path))
        with open(self.path, mode='w', encoding='utf-8') as out_file:
            out_file.write(self.txt)

    def undo(self):
        delete_file(self.path)

class ReadFile:
    def __init__(self, path):
        self.path = path

    def execute(self):
        if verbose:
            print("[reading file '{}']".format(self.path))
        with open(self.path, mode='r', encoding='utf-8') as in_file:
            print(in_file.read(), end='')

def delete_file(path):
    if verbose:
        print("deleting file '{}".format(path))
    os.remove(path)

def main():
    orig_name, new_name = 'file1', 'file2'

    commands = []
    for cmd in CreateFile(orig_name), ReadFile(orig_name), \
RenameFile(orig_name, new_name):
        commands.append(cmd)

    [c.execute() for c in commands]

    answer = input('reverse the executed commands? [y/n] ')


    if answer not in 'yY':
        print("the result is {}".format(new_name))
        exit()
```

```
        for c in reversed(commands):
            try:
                c.undo()
            except AttributeError as e:
                pass

    if __name__ == "__main__":
        main()
```

Let's see two sample executions of command.py. In the first one, there is no undo of commands, whereas in the second one there is:

```
>>> python3 command.py
[creating file 'file1']
[reading file 'file1']
hello world
[renaming 'file1' to 'file2']
reverse the executed commands? [y/n] n
the result is file2

>>> python3 command.py
[creating file 'file1']
[reading file 'file1']
hello world
[renaming 'file1' to 'file2']
reverse the executed commands? [y/n] y
[renaming 'file2' back to 'file1']
deleting file 'file1'
```

The command example can be improved in many aspects. To begin with, none of the utilities follow a defensive programming style [j.mp/dobbdef]. What happens if we try to rename a file that doesn't exist? What about files that exist but cannot be renamed because we don't have the proper filesystem permissions? The same issues exist with all tools; for example, what happens if we try to read a file that doesn't exist? Try improving the utilities by doing some kind of error handling. Is checking the return status of the methods that belong to the os module necessary?

The file creation utility creates a file using the default file permissions as decided by the filesystem. For example, in POSIX systems, the permissions are -rw-rw-r--. You might want to give the ability to the user to provide their own permissions by passing the appropriate parameter to CreateFile. How can you do that? Hint: one way is by using os.fdopen().

And now, here's something for you to think about. I mentioned earlier that a command does not necessarily need to be a class. That's how the delete utility was implemented; there is just a delete_file() function. What are the advantages and disadvantages of this approach? Here's a hint: is it possible to put a delete command in the commands list as it was done for the rest of the commands? We know that functions are first-class citizens in Python, so we can do something such as the following (the first-class.py file):

```
orig_name = 'file1'
df=delete_file

commands = []
commands.append(df)

for c in commands:
    try:
        c.execute()
    except AttributeError as e:
        df(orig_name)

for c in reversed(commands):
    try:
        c.undo()
    except AttributeError as e:
        pass
```

Although this example works, it has some issues:

- The code is not uniform. We rely too much on exception handling, which is not the normal flow of a program. While all the rest of the commands have an execute() method, in this case, there is no execute().

- Currently, the delete file utility has no undo support. What happens if we eventually decide to add undo support for it? Normally, we add an undo() method in the class that represents the command. However, in this case, there is no class. We could create another function to handle undo, but creating a class is a better approach.

Summary

In this chapter, we covered the Command pattern. Using this design pattern, we can encapsulate an operation such as copy/paste as an object. This offers many benefits, as follows:

- We can execute a command whenever we want and not necessarily in creation time
- The client code that executes a command does not need to know any details about how it is implemented
- We can group commands and execute them in a specific order

Executing a command is like ordering at a restaurant. Each customer order is an independent command that enters many stages and is finally executed by the cook.

Many GUI frameworks, including PyQt use the Command pattern to model actions that can be triggered by one or more events and can be customized. However, Command is not limited to frameworks; normal applications such as git-cola also use it for the benefits it offers.

Although the most advertised feature of Command by far is undo, it has more uses. In general, any operation that can be executed on user's will at runtime is a good candidate to use the Command pattern. Command is also great for grouping multiple commands. That's useful for implementing macros, multilevel undo, and transactions. A transaction should either succeed, which means that all operations of it should succeed (the commit operation), or it should fail completely if at least one of its operations fails (the rollback operation). If you want to take the Command pattern to the next level, you can work on an example that involves grouping commands as transactions.

To demonstrate Command, we implemented some basic file utilities on top of Python's os module. Our utilities support undo and have a uniform interface, which makes grouping commands easy.

The next chapter covers the Interpreter pattern, which can be used to create a computer language that focuses on a specific domain. Such a language is called a **Domain Specific Language** (**DSL**).

12
The Interpreter Pattern

There are at least two different user categories for each application:

- **Basic users**: The users of this category just want to be able to use the application in an intuitive way. They don't like to spend too much time on configuring or learning the internals of the application. Basic usage is sufficient for them.

- **Advanced users**: Those users, who are in fact usually the minority, don't mind spending some extra time on learning how to use the advanced features of the application. They can go as far as learning a configuration (or scripting) language if they know that learning it will:

    ° Give them the ability to have better control of an application

    ° Help them express their ideas in a better way

    ° Make them more productive

The **Interpreter** pattern is interesting only for the advanced users of an application. That's because the main idea behind Interpreter is to give the ability to non-beginner users and domain experts to use a simple language to express their ideas. However, what is a simple language? For our needs, a simple language is a language that is less complex than a programming language.

Usually, what we want to create is a **Domain Specific Language** (**DSL**). A DSL is a computer language of limited expressiveness targeting a particular domain. DSLs are used for different things, such as combat simulation, billing, visualization, configuration, communication protocols, and so on. DSLs are divided into internal DSLs and external DSLs [j.mp/wikidsl], [j.mp/fowlerdsl].

Internal DSLs are built on top of a host programming language. An example of an internal DSL is a language that solves linear equations using Python. The advantages of using an internal DSL are that we don't have to worry about creating, compiling, and parsing grammar because these are already taken care of by the host language. The disadvantage is that we are constrained by the features of the host language. It is very challenging to create an expressive, concise, and fluent internal DSL if the host language does not have these features [j.mp/jwodsl].

External DSLs do not depend on host languages. The creator of the DSL can decide all aspects of the language (grammar, syntax, and so forth), but they are also responsible for creating a parser and compiler for it. Creating a parser and compiler for a new language can be a very complex, long, and painful procedure [j.mp/jwodsl].

The Interpreter pattern is related only to internal DSLs. Therefore, our goal is to create a simple but useful language using the features provided by the host programming language, which in this case is Python. Note that Interpreter does not address parsing at all. It assumes that we already have the parsed data in some convenient form. This can be an **abstract syntax tree** (**AST**) or any other handy data structure [GOF95, page 276].

A real-life example

A musician is an example of the Interpreter pattern in reality. Musical notation represents the pitch and duration of a sound graphically. The musician is able to reproduce a sound precisely based on its notation. In a sense, musical notation is the language of music, and the musician is the interpreter of that language. The following figure, which is courtesy of www.sourcemaking.com [j.mp/smintpat], shows a graphical representation of the music example.

A software example

There are many software examples of internal DSLs. PyT is a Python DSL to generate (X)HTML. PyT focuses on performance and claims to have comparable speed with Jinja2 [j.mp/ghpyt]. Of course, we should not assume that the Interpreter pattern is necessarily used in PyT. However, since it is an internal DSL, Interpreter is a very good candidate for it.

Chromium is a FOSS browser that inspired Google Chrome [j.mp/chromiumb]. A part of the Mesa library Python binding of Chromium uses the Interpreter pattern to translate C model arguments to Python objects and executing the related commands [j.mp/intchromium].

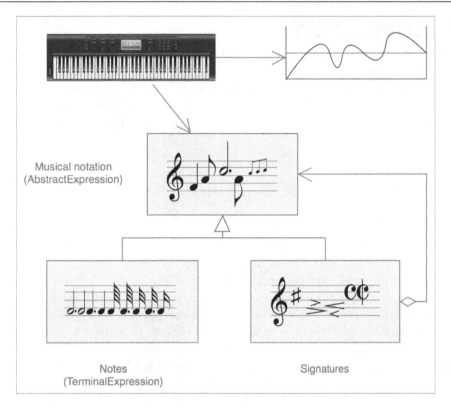

Musical notation
(AbstractExpression)

Notes
(TerminalExpression)

Signatures

Use cases

The Interpreter pattern is used when we want to offer a simple language to domain experts and advanced users to solve their problems. The first thing we should stress is that Interpreter should only be used to implement simple languages. If the language has the requirements of an external DSL, there are better tools to create languages from scratch (yacc and lex, Bison, ANTLR, and so on).

Our goal is to offer the right programming abstractions to the specialist, who is often not a programmer, to make them productive. Ideally, they shouldn't know advanced Python to use our DSL, but knowing even a little bit of Python is a plus since that's what we eventually get at the end. Advanced Python concepts should not be a requirement. Moreover, the performance of the DSL is usually not an important concern. The focus is on offering a language that hides the peculiarities of the host language and offers a more human-readable syntax. Admittedly, Python is already a very readable language with far less peculiar syntax than many other programming languages.

Implementation

Let's create an internal DSL to control a smart house. This example fits well into the Internet of things era, which is getting more and more attention nowadays. The user is able to control their home using a very simple event notation. An event has the form of command -> receiver -> arguments. The arguments part is optional. Not all events require arguments. An example of an event that does not require any arguments is shown:

```
open -> gate
```

An example of an event that requires arguments is shown:

```
increase -> boiler temperature -> 3 degrees
```

The -> symbol is used to mark the end of one part of an event and state the beginning of the next one. There are many ways to implement an internal DSL. We can use plain old regular expressions, string processing, a combination of operator overloading, and metaprogramming, or a library/tool that can do the hard work for us. Although, officially, Interpreter does not address parsing, I feel that a practical example needs to cover parsing as well. For this reason, I decided to use a tool to take care of the parsing part. The tool is called Pyparsing and is part of the standard Python3 distribution. To find out more about Pyparsing, check the mini book *Getting Started with Pyparsing* by Paul McGuire. If Pyparsing is not already installed on your system, you can install it using the following command:

```
>>> pip3 install pyparsing
```

The following sequence diagram shows what happens when the open gate event is executed by the user. The situation is similar for the rest events, with the exception that some events are a bit more complex because they require arguments.

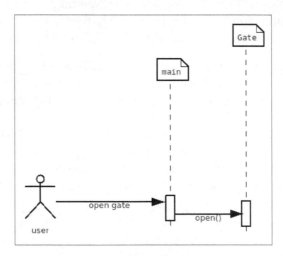

Before getting into coding, it is a good practice to define a simple grammar for our language. We can define the grammar using the **Backus-Naur Form (BNF)** notation [j.mp/bnfgram]:

```
event ::= command token receiver token arguments
command ::= word+
word ::= a collection of one or more alphanumeric characters
token ::= ->
receiver ::= word+
arguments ::= word+
```

What the grammar basically tells us is that an event has the form of command -> receiver -> arguments, and that commands, receivers, and arguments have the same form: a group of one or more alphanumeric characters. If you are wondering about the necessity of the numeric part, it is included to allow us to pass arguments such as **3 degrees** at the command increase -> boiler temperature -> 3 degrees.

Now that we have defined the grammar, we can move on to converting it to actual code. Here's how the code looks:

```
word = Word(alphanums)
command = Group(OneOrMore(word))
token = Suppress("->")
device = Group(OneOrMore(word))
argument = Group(OneOrMore(word))
event = command + token + device + Optional(token + argument)
```

The basic difference between the code and grammar definition is that the code needs to be written in the bottom-up approach. For instance, we cannot use word without first assigning it a value. Suppress is used to state that we want the -> symbol to be skipped from the parsed results.

The full code of this example (the interpreter.py file) uses many placeholder classes, but to keep you focused, I will first show only one class. The complete code listing is also included and will be shown after going through the single class example. Let's take a look at the Boiler class. A boiler has a default temperature of 83 degrees Celsius. There are also two methods to increase and decrease the current temperature:

```python
class Boiler:
    def __init__(self):
        self.temperature = 83 # in celsius

    def __str__(self):
        return 'boiler temperature: {}'.format(self.temperature)
```

```
    def increase_temperature(self, amount):
        print("increasing the boiler's temperature by {}
                degrees".format(amount))
        self.temperature += amount

    def decrease_temperature(self, amount):
        print("decreasing the boiler's temperature by {}
                degrees".format(amount))
        self.temperature -= amount
```

The next step is to add the grammar, which we already covered. We will also create a `boiler` instance and print its default state:

```
word = Word(alphanums)
command = Group(OneOrMore(word))
token = Suppress("->")
device = Group(OneOrMore(word))
argument = Group(OneOrMore(word))
event = command + token + device + Optional(token + argument)

boiler = Boiler()
print(boiler)
```

The simplest way to retrieve the parsed output of Pyparsing is by using the `parseString()` method. The result is a `ParseResults` instance, which is actually a parse tree that can be treated as a nested list. For example, executing `print(event.parseString('increase -> boiler temperature -> 3 degrees'))` gives the following result:

```
[['increase'], ['boiler', 'temperature'], ['3', 'degrees']]
```

So, in this case, we know that the first sublist is the command (increase), the second sublist is the receiver (boiler temperature), and the third sublist is the argument (3 degrees). We can actually unpack the `ParseResults` instance, which gives us direct access to these three parts of the event. Having direct access means that we can match patterns to find out which method should be executed:

```
    cmd, dev, arg = event.parseString('increase -> boiler temperature
-> 3 degrees')
    if 'increase' in ' '.join(cmd):
        if 'boiler' in ' '.join(dev):
            boiler.increase_temperature(int(arg[0]))

    print(boiler)
```

Executing the preceding snippet gives the following output:

```
>>> python3 boiler.py
boiler temperature: 83
increasing the boiler's temperature by 3 degrees
boiler temperature: 86
```

The full code of `interpreter.py` is not very different from what I just described. It is just extended to support more events and devices:

```python
from pyparsing import Word, OneOrMore, Optional, Group, Suppress,
alphanums

class Gate:
    def __init__(self):
        self.is_open = False

    def __str__(self):
        return 'open' if self.is_open else 'closed'

    def open(self):
        print('opening the gate')
        self.is_open = True

    def close(self):
        print('closing the gate')
        self.is_open = False

class Garage:
    def __init__(self):
        self.is_open = False

    def __str__(self):
        return 'open' if self.is_open else 'closed'

    def open(self):
        print('opening the garage')
        self.is_open = True

    def close(self):
        print('closing the garage')
        self.is_open = False
```

```python
class Aircondition:
    def __init__(self):
        self.is_on = False

    def __str__(self):
        return 'on' if self.is_on else 'off'

    def turn_on(self):
        print('turning on the aircondition')
        self.is_on = True

    def turn_off(self):
        print('turning off the aircondition')
        self.is_on = False


class Heating:
    def __init__(self):
        self.is_on = False

    def __str__(self):
        return 'on' if self.is_on else 'off'

    def turn_on(self):
        print('turning on the heating')
        self.is_on = True

    def turn_off(self):
        print('turning off the heating')
        self.is_on = False


class Boiler:
    def __init__(self):
        self.temperature = 83# in celsius

    def __str__(self):
        return 'boiler temperature: {}'.format(self.temperature)

    def increase_temperature(self, amount):
        print("increasing the boiler's temperature by {} degrees".
format(amount))
        self.temperature += amount
```

```python
    def decrease_temperature(self, amount):
        print("decreasing the boiler's temperature by {} degrees".
format(amount))
        self.temperature -= amount

class Fridge:
    def __init__(self):
        self.temperature = 2 # in celsius

    def __str__(self):
        return 'fridge temperature: {}'.format(self.temperature)

    def increase_temperature(self, amount):
        print("increasing the fridge's temperature by {} degrees".
format(amount))
        self.temperature += amount

    def decrease_temperature(self, amount):
        print("decreasing the fridge's temperature by {} degrees".
format(amount))
        self.temperature -= amount


def main():
    word = Word(alphanums)
    command = Group(OneOrMore(word))
    token = Suppress("->")
    device = Group(OneOrMore(word))
    argument = Group(OneOrMore(word))
    event = command + token + device + Optional(token + argument)

    gate = Gate()
    garage = Garage()
    airco = Aircondition()
    heating = Heating()
    boiler = Boiler()
    fridge = Fridge()

    tests = ('open -> gate',
            'close -> garage',
            'turn on -> aircondition',
            'turn off -> heating',
            'increase -> boiler temperature -> 5 degrees',
            'decrease -> fridge temperature -> 2 degrees')
```

```
        open_actions = {'gate':gate.open, 'garage':garage.open,
'aircondition':airco.turn_on,
                    'heating':heating.turn_on, 'boiler
temperature':boiler.increase_temperature,
                    'fridge temperature':fridge.increase_temperature}
        close_actions = {'gate':gate.close, 'garage':garage.close,
'aircondition':airco.turn_off,
                    'heating':heating.turn_off, 'boiler
temperature':boiler.decrease_temperature,
                    'fridge temperature':fridge.decrease_temperature}

    for t in tests:
        if len(event.parseString(t)) == 2: # no argument
            cmd, dev = event.parseString(t)
            cmd_str, dev_str = ' '.join(cmd), ' '.join(dev)
            if 'open' in cmd_str or 'turn on' in cmd_str:
                open_actions[dev_str]()
            elif 'close' in cmd_str or 'turn off' in cmd_str:
                close_actions[dev_str]()
        elif len(event.parseString(t)) == 3: # argument
            cmd, dev, arg = event.parseString(t)
            cmd_str, dev_str, arg_str = ' '.join(cmd), ' '.join(dev),
' '.join(arg)
            num_arg = 0
            try:
                num_arg = int(arg_str.split()[0]) # extract the
numeric part
            except ValueError as err:
                print("expected number but got: '{}'".format(arg_
str[0]))
            if 'increase' in cmd_str and num_arg > 0:
                open_actions[dev_str](num_arg)
            elif 'decrease' in cmd_str and num_arg > 0:
                close_actions[dev_str](num_arg)

if __name__ == '__main__':
    main()
```

Executing the preceding example gives the following output:

```
>>> python3 interpreter.py
opening the gate
closing the garage
turning on the aircondition
turning off the heating
```

```
increasing the boiler's temperature by 5 degrees
decreasing the fridge's temperature by 2 degrees
```

If you want to experiment more with this example, I have a few suggestions for you. The first change that will make it much more interesting is to make it interactive. Currently, all the events are hardcoded in the `tests` tuple. However, the user wants to be able to activate events using an interactive prompt. Do not forget to check how sensitive Pyparsing is regarding spaces, tabs, or unexpected input. For example, what happens if the user types: `turn          off                    ->  heating      37`?

Another possible improvement: notice how the `open_actions` and `close_actions` maps are used to relate a receiver with a method. Is it possible to use a single map instead of two? Are there any advantages in doing that?

Summary

In this chapter, we covered the Interpreter design pattern. The Interpreter pattern is used to offer a programming-like framework to advanced users and domain experts, but without exposing the complexities of a programming language. This is achieved by implementing a DSL.

A DSL is a computer language that has limited expressiveness and targets a specific domain. There are two categories of DSLs: internal DSLs and external DSLs. While internal DSLs are built on top of a host programming language and rely on it, external DSLs are implemented from scratch and do not depend on an existing programming language. Interpreter is related only to internal DSLs.

Musical notation is an example of a non-software DSL. The musician acts as the Interpreter that uses the notation to produce music. From a software perspective, many Python template engines make use of Internal DSLs. PyT is a high-performance Python DSL to generate (X)HTML. We also saw how the Mesa library of Chromium uses the Interpreter pattern to translate graphics-related C code to Python executable objects.

Although parsing is generally not addressed by the Interpreter pattern, in the implementation section, we used Pyparsing to create a DSL that controls a smart house, and saw that using a good parsing tool makes "interpreting" the results using pattern matching simple.

The next chapter demonstrates the Observer pattern. Observer is used to create a publish-subscribe communication type between two or more objects.

13
The Observer Pattern

Sometimes, we want to update a group of objects when the state of another object changes. A very popular example lies in the **Model-View-Controller** (**MVC**) pattern. Assume that we are using the data of the same model in two views, for instance in a pie chart and in a spreadsheet. Whenever the model is modified, both the views need to be updated. That's the role of the Observer design pattern [Eckel08, page 213].

The Observer pattern describes a publish-subscribe relationship between a single object, : the publisher, which is also known as the subject or observable, and one or more objects, : the subscribers, also known as observers. In the MVC example, the publisher is the model and the subscribers are the views. However, MVC is not the only publish-subscribe example. Subscribing to a news feed such as RSS or Atom is another example. Many readers can subscribe to the feed typically using a feed reader, and every time a new item is added, they receive the update automatically.

The ideas behind Observer are the same as the ideas behind MVC and the separation of concerns principle, that is, to increase decoupling between the publisher and subscribers, and to make it easy to add/remove subscribers at runtime. Additionally, the publisher is not concerned about who its observers are. It just sends notifications to all the subscribers [GOF95, page 327].

A real-life example

In reality, an auction resembles Observer. Every auction bidder has a number paddle that is raised whenever they want to place a bid. Whenever the paddle is raised by a bidder, the auctioneer acts as the subject by updating the price of the bid and broadcasting the new price to all bidders (subscribers).

The following figure, courtesy of `www.sourcemaking.com`, [`j.mp/observerpat`], shows how the Observer pattern relates to an auction:

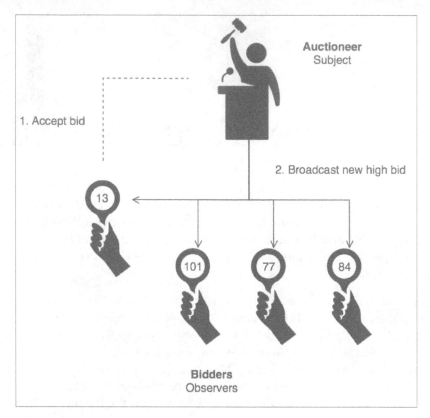

A software example

The django-observer package [`j.mp/django-obs`] is a third-party Django package that can be used to register callback functions that are executed when there are changes in several Django fields. Many different types of fields are supported (`CharField`, `IntegerField`, and so forth).

RabbitMQ is a library that can be used to add asynchronous messaging support to an application. Several messaging protocols are supported, such as HTTP and AMQP. RabbitMQ can be used in a Python application to implement a publish-subscribe pattern, which is nothing more than the Observer design pattern [`j.mp/rabbitmqobs`].

Use cases

We generally use the Observer pattern when we want to inform/update one or more objects (observers/subscribers) about a change that happened to another object (subject/publisher/observable). The number of observers as well as who the observers are may vary and can be changed dynamically (at runtime).

We can think of many cases where Observer can be useful. One such case was already mentioned at the start of this chapter: news feeds. Whether it is RSS, Atom, or another format, the idea is the same; you follow a feed, and every time it is updated, you receive a notification about the update [Zlobin13, page 60].

The same concept exists in social networking. If you are connected to another person using a social networking service, and your connection updates something, you are notified about it. It doesn't matter if the connection is a Twitter user that you follow, a real friend on Facebook, or a business colleague on LinkedIn.

Event-driven systems are another example where Observer can be (and usually is) used. In such systems, listeners are used to "listen" for specific events. The listeners are triggered when an event they are listening to is created. This can be typing a specific key (of the keyboard), moving the mouse, and more. The event plays the role of the publisher and the listeners play the role of the observers. The key point in this case is that multiple listeners (observers) can be attached to a single event (publisher) [j.mp/magobs].

Implementation

In this section, we will implement a data formatter. The ideas described here are based on the ActiveState Python Observer code recipe [j.mp/pythonobs]. There is a default formatter that shows a value in the decimal format. However, we can add/register more formatters. In this example, we will add a hex and binary formatter. Every time the value of the default formatter is updated, the registered formatters are notified and take action. In this case, the action is to show the new value in the relevant format.

Observer is actually one of the patterns where inheritance makes sense. We can have a base `Publisher` class that contains the common functionality of adding, removing, and notifying observers. Our `DefaultFormatter` class derives from `Publisher` and adds the formatter-specific functionality. We can dynamically add and remove observers on demand. The following class diagram shows an instance of the example using two observers: `HexFormatter` and `BinaryFormatter`. Note that, because class diagrams are static, they cannot show the whole lifetime of a system, only the state of it at a specific point in time.

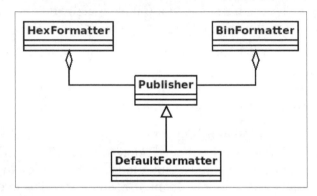

We begin with the `Publisher` class. The observers are kept in the `observers` list. The `add()` method registers a new observer, or throws an error if it already exists. The `remove()` method unregisters an existing observer, or throws an exception if it does not exist. Finally, the `notify()` method informs all observers about a change:

```python
class Publisher:
    def __init__(self):
        self.observers = []

    def add(self, observer):
        if observer not in self.observers:
            self.observers.append(observer)
        else:
            print('Failed to add: {}'.format(observer))

    def remove(self, observer):
        try:
            self.observers.remove(observer)
        except ValueError:
            print('Failed to remove: {}'.format(observer))

    def notify(self):
        [o.notify(self) for o in self.observers]
```

Let's continue with the `DefaultFormatter` class. The first thing that `__init__()` does is call `__init__()` method of the base class, since this is not done automatically in Python. A `DefaultFormatter` instance has name to make it easier for us to track its status. We use name mangling in the `_data` variable to state that it should not be accessed directly. Note that this is always possible in Python [Lott14, page 54] but fellow developers have no excuse for doing so, since the code already states that they shouldn't. There is a serious reason for using name mangling in this case. Stay tuned. `DefaultFormatter` treats the `_data` variable as an integer, and the default value is zero:

```python
class DefaultFormatter(Publisher):
    def __init__(self, name):
        Publisher.__init__(self)
        self.name = name
        self._data = 0
```

The `__str__()` method returns information about the name of the publisher and the value of `_data`. `type(self).__name__` is a handy trick to get the name of a class without hardcoding it. It is one of those things that make the code less readable but easier to maintain. It is up to you to decide if you like it or not:

```python
def __str__(self):
        return "{}: '{}' has data = {}".format(type(self).__name__,
self.name,

self._data)
```

There are two `data()` methods. The first one uses the `@property` decorator to give read access to the `_data` variable. Using this, we can just execute `object.data` instead of `object.data()`:

```python
    @property
    def data(self):
        return self._data
```

The second `data()` method is more interesting. It uses the `@setter` decorator, which is called every time the assignment (=) operator is used to assign a new value to the `_data` variable. This method also tries to cast a new value to an integer, and does exception handling in case this operation fails:

```python
    @data.setter
    def data(self, new_value):
        try:
            self._data = int(new_value)
        except ValueError as e:
```

```
                    print('Error: {}'.format(e))
            else:
                    self.notify()
```

The next step is to add the observers. The functionality of `HexFormatter` and `BinaryFormatter` is very similar. The only difference between them is how they format the value of data received by the publisher, that is, in hexadecimal and binary, respectively:

```
class HexFormatter:
    def notify(self, publisher):
        print("{}: '{}' has now hex data = {}".format(type(self).__
name__,
                    publisher.name, hex(publisher.data)))


class BinaryFormatter:
    def notify(self, publisher):
        print("{}: '{}' has now bin data = {}".format(type(self).__
name__,
                    publisher.name, bin(publisher.data)))
```

No example is fun without some test data. The `main()` function initially creates a `DefaultFormatter` instance named `test1` and afterwards attaches (and detaches) the two available observers. Exception handling is also exercised to make sure that the application does not crash when erroneous data is passed by the user. Moreover, things such as trying to add the same observer twice or removing an observer that does not exist should cause no crashes:

```
def main():
    df = DefaultFormatter('test1')
    print(df)

    print()
    hf = HexFormatter()
    df.add(hf)
    df.data = 3
    print(df)

    print()
    bf = BinaryFormatter()
    df.add(bf)
    df.data = 21
    print(df)
```

```
    print()
    df.remove(hf)
    df.data = 40
    print(df)

    print()
    df.remove(hf)
    df.add(bf)

    df.data = 'hello'
    print(df)

    print()
    df.data = 15.8
    print(df)
```

Here's how the full code of the example (observer.py) looks:

```
class Publisher:
    def __init__(self):
        self.observers = []

    def add(self, observer):
        if observer not in self.observers:
            self.observers.append(observer)
        else:
            print('Failed to add: {}'.format(observer))

    def remove(self, observer):
        try:
            self.observers.remove(observer)
        except ValueError:
            print('Failed to remove: {}'.format(observer))

    def notify(self):
        [o.notify(self) for o in self.observers]

class DefaultFormatter(Publisher):
    def __init__(self, name):
        Publisher.__init__(self)
        self.name = name
        self._data = 0
```

```python
    def __str__(self):
        return "{}: '{}' has data = {}".format(type(self).__name__,
self.name, self._data)

    @property
    def data(self):
        return self._data

    @data.setter
    def data(self, new_value):
        try:
            self._data = int(new_value)
        except ValueError as e:
            print('Error: {}'.format(e))
        else:
            self.notify()


class HexFormatter:
    def notify(self, publisher):
        print("{}: '{}' has now hex data = {}".format(type(self).__
name__, publisher.name, hex(publisher.data)))


class BinaryFormatter:
    def notify(self, publisher):
        print("{}: '{}' has now bin data = {}".format(type(self).__
name__, publisher.name, bin(publisher.data)))


def main():
    df = DefaultFormatter('test1')
    print(df)

    print()
    hf = HexFormatter()
    df.add(hf)
    df.data = 3
    print(df)

    print()
    bf = BinaryFormatter()
    df.add(bf)
    df.data = 21
    print(df)

    print()
    df.remove(hf)
    df.data = 40
    print(df)
```

```
        print()
        df.remove(hf)
        df.add(bf)

        df.data = 'hello'
        print(df)

        print()
        df.data = 15.8
        print(df)

    if __name__ == '__main__':
        main()
```

Executing observer.py gives the following output:

```
>>> python3 observer.py
DefaultFormatter: 'test1' has data = 0


HexFormatter: 'test1' has now hex data = 0x3
DefaultFormatter: 'test1' has data = 3


HexFormatter: 'test1' has now hex data = 0x15
BinaryFormatter: 'test1' has now bin data = 0b10101
DefaultFormatter: 'test1' has data = 21


BinaryFormatter: 'test1' has now bin data = 0b101000
DefaultFormatter: 'test1' has data = 40


Failed to remove: <__main__.HexFormatter object at 0x7f30a2fb82e8>
Failed to add: <__main__.BinaryFormatter object at 0x7f30a2fb8320>
Error: invalid literal for int() with base 10: 'hello'
BinaryFormatter: 'test1' has now bin data = 0b101000
DefaultFormatter: 'test1' has data = 40


BinaryFormatter: 'test1' has now bin data = 0b1111
DefaultFormatter: 'test1' has data = 15
```

What we see in the output is that as the extra observers are added, more (and relevant) output is shown, and when an observer is removed, it is not notified any longer. That's exactly what we want: runtime notifications that we are able to enable/disable on demand.

The defensive programming part of the application also seems to work fine. Trying to do funny things such as removing an observer that does not exist or adding the same observer twice is not allowed. The messages shown are not very user-friendly but I leave that up to you as an exercise. Runtime failures of trying to pass a string when the API expects a number are also properly handled without causing the application to crash/terminate.

This example would be much more interesting if it were interactive. Even a simple menu that allows the user to attach/detach observers at runtime and modify the value of `DefaultFormatter` would be nice because the runtime aspect becomes much more visible. Feel free to do it.

Another nice exercise is to add more observers. For example, you can add an octal formatter, a roman numeral formatter, or any other observer that uses your favorite representation. Be creative and have fun!

Summary

In this chapter, we covered the Observer design pattern. We use Observer when we want to be able to inform/notify all stakeholders (an object or a group of objects) when the state of an object changes. An important feature of observer is that the number of subscribers/observers as well as who the subscribers are may vary and can be changed at runtime.

To understand Observer, you can think of an auction, with the bidders being the subscribers and the auctioneer being the publisher. This pattern is used quite a lot in the software world.

In general, all systems that make use of the MVC pattern are event-based. As specific examples, we mentioned:

- django-observer, a third-party Django library used to register observers that are executed when fields are modified.
- The Python bindings of RabbitMQ. We referred to a specific example of RabbitMQ used to implement the publish-subscribe (aka Observer) pattern.

In the implementation example, we saw how to use Observer to create data formatters that can be attached and detached at runtime to enrich the behavior of an object. Hopefully, you will find the recommended exercises interesting.

The next chapter introduces the State design pattern, which can be used to implement a core computer science concept: state machines.

14
The State Pattern

Object-oriented programming focuses on mutating the state of objects that interact with each other. A very handy tool to model (and when necessary, mathematically formalize) state transitions in many problems is using a finite-state machine (commonly known as a state machine) First, what's a state machine? A state machine is an abstract machine that has two key components: states and transitions. A state is the current (active) status of a system. For example, if we have a radio receiver, two possible states are tuning on the FM or AM. Another possible state is switching from one FM/AM radio station to another. A transition is the switch from one state to another. A transition is initiated by a triggering event or condition. Usually, an action or set of actions is executed before or after a transition occurs. Assuming that our radio receiver is tuned on the 107 FM station, an example of a transition is the button pressed by the listener to switch to 107.5 FM.

A nice feature of state machines is that they can be represented as graphs (called state diagrams), where each state is a node and each transition is an edge between two nodes. The following figure, courtesy of Wikipedia [j.mp/wikistate], shows the state diagram of a typical operating system process (no specific systems are targeted). When a process is initially created by a user, it goes into the *created/new* state. From this state, the only transition is to go into the *waiting* state, which happens when the scheduler loads the process in memory and adds it to the queue of the processes that are *waiting/ready for execution*. A *waiting* process has two possible transitions: it can either be picked for execution (transition to *running*), or it can be replaced with a process that has higher priority (transition to *swapped out and waiting*).

Other typical states of a process are *terminated* (completed or killed), *blocked* (for example, waiting for an I/O operation to complete), and so forth. It is important to note that a state machine has only one active state at a specific point in time. For instance, a process cannot be at the same time in the state *created* and the state *running*.

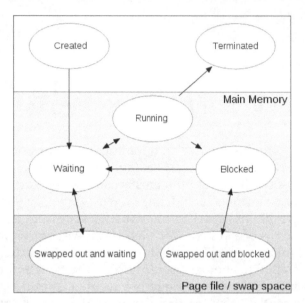

State machines can be used to solve many kinds of different problems, including non-computational problems. Non-computational examples include vending machines, elevators, traffic lights, combination locks, parking meters, automated gas pumps, and natural language grammar description. Computational examples include game programming and other domains of computer programming, hardware design, protocol design, and programming language parsing [j.mp/ wikifsm], [j.mp/fsmfound].

Alright, that sounds good. But how are state machines related to the **State design pattern**? It turns out that the State pattern is nothing more than a state machine applied on a particular Software Engineering problem [GOF95, page 342], [Eckel08, page 151].

A real-life example

Once again (we saw this in the Chain of Responsibility pattern), a snack vending machine is an example of the State pattern in everyday life. Vending machines have different states and react differently depending on the amount of money that we insert. Depending on our selection and the money we inserted, the machine can:

- Reject our selection because the product we requested is out of stock
- Reject our selection because the amount of money we inserted is not sufficient
- Deliver the product and give no change because we inserted the exact amount
- Deliver the product and return the change

There are, for sure, more possible states, but you get the point. The following figure, provided by www.sourcemaking.com [j.mp/smstate], shows a possible implementation of the different vending machine states using inheritance:

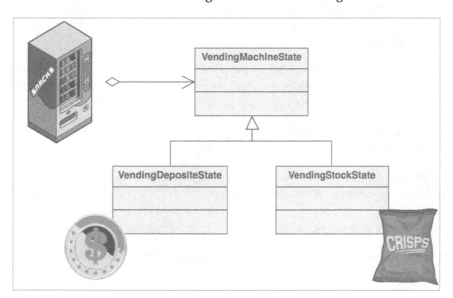

A software example

Using the State pattern in essence means implementing a state machine to solve a software problem in a specific domain. The django-fsm package is a third-party package that can be used to simplify the implementation and usage of state machines in the Django framework [j.mp/django-fsm].

Python offers more than one third-party package/module to use and implement state machines [j.mp/pyfsm]. We will see how to use one of them in the implementation section.

Another project worth mentioning is the State Machine Compiler (SMC). With SMC, you can describe your state machine in a single text file using a simple **Domain Specific Language (DSL)**, and it will generate the state machine's code automatically. The project claims that the DSL is so simple that you can write it as a one-to-one translation of a state diagram. I haven't tried it but that sounds very interesting. SMC can generate code in a number of programming languages, including Python [j.mp/smcsrc].

Use cases

The State pattern is applicable to many problems. All the problems that can be solved using state machines are good use cases to use the State pattern. An example we have already seen is the process model of an operating/embedded system.

Programming language compiler implementation is another good example. Lexical and syntactic analysis can use states to build abstract syntax trees [j.mp/wikifsm].

Event-driven systems are yet another example. In an event-driven system, the transition from one state to another triggers an event/message. Many computer games use this technique. For example, a monster might move from the state guard to the state attack when the main hero approaches it [j.mp/wikievfsm], [j.mp/gamefsm].

To quote Thomas Jaeger: *"the state design pattern allows for full encapsulation of an unlimited number of states on a context for easy maintenance and flexibility"* [j.mp/statevs].

Implementation

Let's write the required Python code that demonstrates how to create a state machine based on the state diagram shown earlier in this chapter. Our state machine should cover the different states of a process and the transitions between them.

The State design pattern is usually implemented using a parent `State` class that contains the common functionality of all the states, and a number of derived `ConcreteState` classes, where each derived class contains only the state-specific required functionality. A sample implementation can be found at [`j.mp/statepat`]. In my opinion, these are implementation details. The State pattern focuses on implementing a state machine. The core parts of a state machine are the states and transitions between the states. It doesn't matter how those parts are implemented.

To avoid reinventing the wheel, we can make use of the existing Python modules that not only help us create state machines, but also do it in a Pythonic way. A module that I find very useful is `state_machine` [`j.mp/state_machine`]. Before going any further, if `state_machine` is not already installed on your system, you can install it using the following command:

```
>>>   pip3 install state_machine
```

The `state_machine` module is simple enough that no special introduction is required. We will cover most aspects of it while going through the code of the example.

Let's start with the `Process` class. Each created process has its own state machine. The first step to create a state machine using the `state_machine` module is to use the `@acts_as_state_machine` decorator:

```
@acts_as_state_machine
class Process:
```

Next, we define the states of our state machine. This is a one-to-one mapping of what we see in the state diagram. The only difference is that we should give a hint about the initial state of the state machine. We do that by setting `initial=True`:

```
created = State(initial=True)
waiting = State()
running = State()
terminated = State()
blocked = State()
swapped_out_waiting = State()
swapped_out_blocked = State()
```

We continue with defining the transitions. In the `state_machine` module, a transition has the name `Event`. We define the possible transitions using the arguments `from_states` and `to_state`. `from_states` can be either a single state or a group of states (tuple):

```
wait = Event(from_states=(created, running, blocked,
                          swapped_out_waiting), to_state=waiting)
```

```
    run = Event(from_states=waiting, to_state=running)
    terminate = Event(from_states=running, to_state=terminated)
    block = Event(from_states=(running, swapped_out_blocked),
                        to_state=blocked)
    swap_wait = Event(from_states=waiting, to_state=swapped_out_
waiting)
    swap_block = Event(from_states=blocked, to_state=swapped_out_
blocked)
```

Each process has a name. Officially, a process needs to have much more information to be useful (for example, ID, priority, status, and so forth) but let's keep it simple to focus on the pattern:

```
def __init__(self, name):
    self.name = name
```

Transitions are not very useful if nothing happens when they occur. The state_machine module provides us with the @before and @after decorators that can be used to execute actions before or after a transition occurs, respectfully. For the purpose of this example, the actions are limited to printing information about the state change of the process:

```
@after('wait')
def wait_info(self):
    print('{} entered waiting mode'.format(self.name))


@after('run')
def run_info(self):
    print('{} is running'.format(self.name))

@before('terminate')
def terminate_info(self):
    print('{} terminated'.format(self.name))

@after('block')
def block_info(self):
    print('{} is blocked'.format(self.name))

@after('swap_wait')
def swap_wait_info(self):
    print('{} is swapped out and waiting'.format(self.name))

@after('swap_block')
def swap_block_info(self):
    print('{} is swapped out and blocked'.format(self.name))
```

The `transition()` function accepts three arguments: `process`, which is an instance of `Process`, `event`, which is an instance of `Event` (`wait`, `run`, `terminate`, and so forth), and `event_name`, which is the name of the event. The name of the event is printed if something goes wrong when trying to execute `event`:

```
def transition(process, event, event_name):
    try:
        event()
    except  InvalidStateTransition as err:
        print('Error: transition of {} from {} to {} failed'.
format(process.name,
                process.current_state, event_name))
```

The `state_info()` function shows some basic information about the current (active) state of the process:

```
def state_info(process):
    print('state of {}: {}'.format(process.name, process.current_
state))
```

At the beginning of the `main()` function, we define some string constants, which are passed as `event_name`:

```
def main():
    RUNNING = 'running'
    WAITING = 'waiting'
    BLOCKED = 'blocked'
    TERMINATED = 'terminated'
```

Next, we create two `Process` instances and print information about their initial state:

```
    p1, p2 = Process('process1'), Process('process2')
    [state_info(p) for p in (p1, p2)]
```

The rest of the function experiments with different transitions. Recall the state diagram we covered in this chapter. The allowed transitions should be with respect to the state diagram. For example, it should be possible to switch from state *running* to state *blocked*, but it shouldn't be possible to switch from state *blocked* to state *running*:

```
    print()
    transition(p1, p1.wait, WAITING)
    transition(p2, p2.terminate, TERMINATED)
    [state_info(p) for p in (p1, p2)]

    print()
    transition(p1, p1.run, RUNNING)
```

```
        transition(p2, p2.wait, WAITING)
        [state_info(p) for p in (p1, p2)]

        print()
        transition(p2, p2.run, RUNNING)
        [state_info(p) for p in (p1, p2)]

        print()
        [transition(p, p.block, BLOCKED) for p in (p1, p2)]
        [state_info(p) for p in (p1, p2)]

        print()
        [transition(p, p.terminate, TERMINATED) for p in (p1, p2)]
        [state_info(p) for p in (p1, p2)]
```

Here is the full code of the example (the state.py file):

```
from state_machine import State, Event, acts_as_state_machine, after,
before, InvalidStateTransition


@acts_as_state_machine
class Process:
    created = State(initial=True)
    waiting = State()
    running = State()
    terminated = State()
    blocked = State()
    swapped_out_waiting = State()
    swapped_out_blocked = State()


    wait = Event(from_states=(created, running, blocked,
                            swapped_out_waiting), to_state=waiting)
    run = Event(from_states=waiting, to_state=running)
    terminate = Event(from_states=running, to_state=terminated)
    block = Event(from_states=(running, swapped_out_blocked),
                            to_state=blocked)
    swap_wait = Event(from_states=waiting, to_state=swapped_out_
waiting)
    swap_block = Event(from_states=blocked, to_state=swapped_out_
blocked)


    def __init__(self, name):
        self.name = name
```

```python
    @after('wait')
    def wait_info(self):
        print('{} entered waiting mode'.format(self.name))

    @after('run')
    def run_info(self):
        print('{} is running'.format(self.name))

    @before('terminate')
    def terminate_info(self):
        print('{} terminated'.format(self.name))

    @after('block')
    def block_info(self):
        print('{} is blocked'.format(self.name))

    @after('swap_wait')
    def swap_wait_info(self):
        print('{} is swapped out and waiting'.format(self.name))

    @after('swap_block')
    def swap_block_info(self):
        print('{} is swapped out and blocked'.format(self.name))

def transition(process, event, event_name):
    try:
        event()
    except  InvalidStateTransition as err:
        print('Error: transition of {} from {} to {} failed'.
format(process.name,
                    process.current_state, event_name))

def state_info(process):
    print('state of {}: {}'.format(process.name, process.current_
state))

def main():
    RUNNING = 'running'
    WAITING = 'waiting'
    BLOCKED = 'blocked'
    TERMINATED = 'terminated'

    p1, p2 = Process('process1'), Process('process2')
    [state_info(p) for p in (p1, p2)]
```

```
        print()
        transition(p1, p1.wait, WAITING)
        transition(p2, p2.terminate, TERMINATED)
        [state_info(p) for p in (p1, p2)]

        print()
        transition(p1, p1.run, RUNNING)
        transition(p2, p2.wait, WAITING)
        [state_info(p) for p in (p1, p2)]

        print()
        transition(p2, p2.run, RUNNING)
        [state_info(p) for p in (p1, p2)]

        print()
        [transition(p, p.block, BLOCKED) for p in (p1, p2)]
        [state_info(p) for p in (p1, p2)]

        print()
        [transition(p, p.terminate, TERMINATED) for p in (p1, p2)]
        [state_info(p) for p in (p1, p2)]

    if __name__ == '__main__':
        main()
```

Here's what we get when executing state.py:

```
>>> python3 state.py
state of process1: created
state of process2: created

process1 entered waiting mode
Error: transition of process2 from created to terminated failed
state of process1: waiting
state of process2: created

process1 is running
process2 entered waiting mode
state of process1: running
state of process2: waiting
```

```
process2 is running
state of process1: running
state of process2: running

process1 is blocked
process2 is blocked
state of process1: blocked
state of process2: blocked

Error: transition of process1 from blocked to terminated failed
Error: transition of process2 from blocked to terminated failed
state of process1: blocked
state of process2: blocked
```

Indeed, the output shows that illegal transitions such as *created* → *terminated* and *blocked* → *terminated* fail gracefully. We don't want the application to crash when an illegal transition is requested, and this is handled properly by the except block.

Notice how using a good module such as state_machine eliminates conditional logic. There's no need to use long and error-prone if-else statements that check for each and every state transition and react upon them.

To get a better feeling about the State pattern and state machines, I strongly recommend you to implement your own example. This can be anything, a simple video game (you can use state machines to handle the states of the main hero and the enemies), an elevator, a parser, or any other system that can be modeled using state machines.

Summary

In this chapter, we covered the State design pattern. The State pattern is an implementation of one or more finite-state machines (in short, state machines) used to solve a particular Software Engineering problem.

A state machine is an abstract machine with two main components: states and transitions. A state is the current status of a system. A state machine can have only one active state at any point in time. A transition is a switch from the current state to a new state. It is normal to execute one or more actions before or after a transition occurs. State machines can be represented visually using state diagrams.

State machines are used to solve many computational and non-computational problems. Some of them are traffic lights, parking meters, hardware design, programming language parsing, and so forth. We saw how a snack vending machine relates to the way a state machine works.

Modern software offers libraries/modules to make the implementation and usage of state machines easier. Django offers the third-party django-fsm package and Python also has many contributed modules. In fact, one of them (`state_machine`) was used in the implementation section. The **State Machine Compiler (SMC)** is yet another promising project, offering many programming language bindings (including Python).

We saw how to implement a state machine of a computer system process using the `state_machine` module. The `state_machine` module simplifies the creation of a state machine and the definition of actions before/after transitions.

In the next chapter, we will see how we can pick an algorithm (between many candidates) dynamically using the Strategy design pattern.

15
The Strategy Pattern

Most problems can be solved in more than one way. Take, for example, the sorting problem, which is related to putting the elements of a list in a specific order. There are many sorting algorithms, and, in general, none of them is considered the best for all cases [j.mp/algocomp]. There are different criteria that help us pick a sorting algorithm on a per-case basis. Some of the things that should be taken into account are:

- **Number of elements that need to be sorted**: This is called the input size. Almost all the sorting algorithms behave fairly well when the input size is small, but only a few of them have good performance with a large input size.

- **Best/average/worst time complexity of the algorithm**: Time complexity is (roughly) the amount of time the algorithm takes to complete, excluding coefficients and lower order terms. This is often the most usual criterion to pick an algorithm, although it is not always sufficient.

- **Space complexity of the algorithm**: Space complexity is (again roughly) the amount of physical memory needed to fully execute an algorithm. This is very important when we are working with big data or embedded systems, which usually have limited memory.

- **Stability of the algorithm**: An algorithm is considered stable when it maintains the relative order of elements with equal values after it is executed.

- **Code complexity of the algorithm**: If two algorithms have the same time/space complexity and are both stable, it is important to know which algorithm is easier to code and maintain.

There are possibly more criteria that can be taken into account. The important question is are we really forced to use a single sorting algorithm for all cases? The answer is of course not. A better solution is to have all the sorting algorithms available, and using the mentioned criteria to pick the best algorithm for the current case. That's what the Strategy pattern is about.

The **Strategy pattern** promotes using multiple algorithms to solve a problem. Its killer feature is that it makes it possible to switch algorithms at runtime transparently (the client code is unaware of the change). So, if you have two algorithms and you know that one works better with small input sizes, while the other works better with large input sizes, you can use Strategy to decide which algorithm to use based on the input data at runtime.

A real-life example

Reaching an airport to catch a flight is a good Strategy example used in reality:

- If we want to save money and we leave early, we can go by bus/train
- If we don't mind paying for a parking place and have our own car, we can go by car
- If we don't have a car but we are in a hurry, we can take a taxi

There are trade-offs between cost, time, convenience, and so forth. The following figure, courtesy of `www.sourcemaking.com` [`j.mp/strategypat`], shows an example of the different ways (strategies) you can reach the airport:

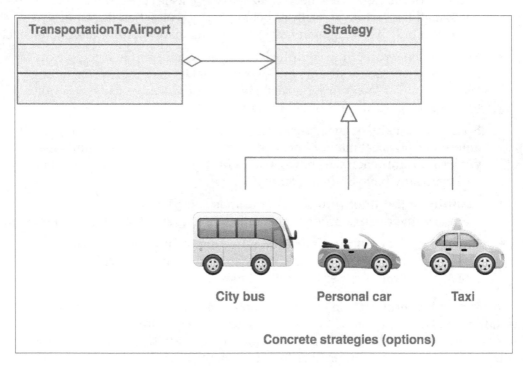

A software example

Python's `sorted()` and `list.sort()` functions are examples of the Strategy pattern. Both functions accept a named parameter `key`, which is basically the name of the function that implements a sorting Strategy [Eckel08, page 202].

The following example (the code is in the `langs.py` file) shows how two different strategies can be used to sort programming languages in the following ways:

- Alphabetically
- Based on their popularity (using the TIOBE index [j.mp/tiobe14])

A `namedtuple` programming language [j.mp/namedtuple] is used to keep the statistics of the programming languages. A named tuple is an easy-to-create, lightweight, immutable object type. It is compatible with a normal `tuple` but it can also be treated as an object (can be called by name, using the usual class notation). A named tuple can be used [j.mp/sonamed]:

- Instead of a class when we want to focus on immutability
- Instead of a tuple, when it makes sense to use the object notation to create more readable code

I took the liberty to also demonstrate the `pprint` and `attrgetter` modules. The `pprint` module is used to pretty print a data structure, and `attregetter` is used to access the attributes of `class` or `namedtuple` by name. The alternative of using `attregetter` is to use a `lambda` function, but I find `attregetter` more readable:

```
import pprint
from collections import namedtuple
from operator import attrgetter

if __name__ == '__main__':
    ProgrammingLang = namedtuple('ProgrammingLang', 'name ranking')

    stats = ( ('Ruby', 14), ('Javascript', 8), ('Python', 7),
                ('Scala', 31), ('Swift', 18), ('Lisp', 23) )

    lang_stats = [ProgrammingLang(n, r) for n, r in stats]
    pp = pprint.PrettyPrinter(indent=5)
    pp.pprint(sorted(lang_stats, key=attrgetter('name')))
    print()
    pp.pprint(sorted(lang_stats, key=attrgetter('ranking')))
```

Executing `langs.py` gives the following output:

```
>>>python3 langs.py
[    ProgrammingLang(name='Javascript', ranking=8),
     ProgrammingLang(name='Lisp', ranking=23),
     ProgrammingLang(name='Python', ranking=7),
     ProgrammingLang(name='Ruby', ranking=14),
     ProgrammingLang(name='Scala', ranking=31),
     ProgrammingLang(name='Swift', ranking=18)]


[    ProgrammingLang(name='Python', ranking=7),
     ProgrammingLang(name='Javascript', ranking=8),
     ProgrammingLang(name='Ruby', ranking=14),
     ProgrammingLang(name='Swift', ranking=18),
     ProgrammingLang(name='Lisp', ranking=23),
     ProgrammingLang(name='Scala', ranking=31)]
```

The Java API also uses the Strategy design pattern. The `java.util.Comparator` is an interface that contains a `compare()` method, which is essentially a strategy that can be passed to sorting methods such as `Collections.sort` and `Arrays.sort` [`j.mp/jdkpatterns`].

Use cases

Strategy is a very generic design pattern with many use cases. In general, whenever we want to be able to apply different algorithms dynamically and transparently, Strategy is the way to go. By different algorithms, I mean different implementations of the same algorithm. This means that the result should be exactly the same, but each implementation has a different performance and code complexity (as an example, think of sequential search versus binary search).

We have already seen how Python and Java use the Strategy pattern to support different sorting algorithms. However, Strategy is not limited to sorting. It can also be used to create all kinds of different resource filters (authentication, logging, data compression, encryption, and so forth) [`j.mp/javaxfilter`].

Another usage of the Strategy pattern is to create different formatting representations, either to achieve portability (for example, line-breaking differences between platforms) or dynamically change the representation of data.

Yet another usage of Strategy worth mentioning is in simulations. If we want, for instance, to simulate robots, we know that some robots are more aggressive than others, some are faster, and so forth. All these differences in robot behavior can be modeled as different Strategies [j.mp/oostrat].

Implementation

There is not much to be said about implementing the Strategy pattern. In languages where functions are not first-class citizens, each Strategy should be implemented in a different class. Wikipedia demonstrates that at [j.mp/stratwiki]. In Python, we can treat functions as normal variables and this simplifies the implementation of Strategy.

Assume that we are asked to implement an algorithm to check if all characters in a string are unique. For example, the algorithm should return true if we enter the string "dream" because none of the characters is repeated. If we enter the string "pizza", it should return false because the letter "z" exists two times. Note that the repeated characters do not need to be consecutive, and the string does not need to be a valid word. The algorithm should also return false for the string "1r2a3ae" because the letter "a" appears twice.

After thinking about the problem carefully, we come up with an implementation that sorts the string and compares all characters pair by pair. First, we implement the pairs() function, which returns all neighbor pairs of a sequence seq.

```
def pairs(seq):
    n = len(seq)
    for i in range(n):
        yield seq[i], seq[(i + 1) % n]
```

Next, we implement the allUniqueSort() function, which accepts a string s and returns True if all characters in the string are unique; otherwise, it returns False. To demonstrate the Strategy pattern, we will make a simplification by assuming that this algorithm fails to scale. We assume that it works fine for strings that are up to five characters. For longer strings, we simulate a slowdown by inserting a sleep statement:

```
SLOW = 3                    # in seconds
LIMIT = 5                   # in characters
WARNING = 'too bad, you picked the slow algorithm :('

def allUniqueSort(s):
    if len(s) > LIMIT:
        print(WARNING)
        time.sleep(SLOW)
```

```
        srtStr = sorted(s)
        for (c1, c2) in pairs(srtStr):
            if c1 == c2:
                return False
        return True
```

We are not happy with the performance of `allUniqueSort()` and we are trying to think of ways to improve it. After some time, we come up with a new algorithm `allUniqueSet()` that eliminates the need to sort. In this case, we use a set. If the character in check has already been inserted in the set, it means that not all characters in the string are unique:

```
def allUniqueSet(s):
    if len(s) < LIMIT:
        print(WARNING)
        time.sleep(SLOW)

    return True if len(set(s)) == len(s) else False
```

Unfortunately, while `allUniqueSet()` has no scaling problems, for some strange reason, it has worse performance than `allUniqueSort()` when checking short strings. What can we do in this case? Well, we can keep both algorithms and use the one that fits best, depending on the length of the string that we want to check. The function `allUnique()` accepts an input string s and a strategy function `strategy`, which in this case is one of `allUniqueSort()`, `allUniqueSet()`. The function `allUnique()` executes the input strategy and returns its result to the caller.

The `main()` function lets the user:

- Enter the word to be checked for character uniqueness
- Choose the pattern that will be used

It also does some basic error handling and gives the ability to the user to quit gracefully:

```
def main():
    while True:
        word = None
        while not word:
            word = input('Insert word (type quit to exit)> ')

            if word == 'quit':
                print('bye')
                return
```

```
                strategy_picked = None
                strategies = { '1': allUniqueSet, '2': allUniqueSort }
                while strategy_picked not in strategies.keys():
                    strategy_picked = input('Choose strategy: [1] Use a
set, [2] Sort and pair> ')

                try:
                    strategy = strategies[strategy_picked]
                    print('allUnique({}): {}'.format(word,
allUnique(word, strategy)))
                except KeyError as err:
                    print('Incorrect option: {}'.format(strategy_
picked))
```

Here's the complete code of the example (the `strategy.py` file):

```python
import time

SLOW = 3                        # in seconds
LIMIT = 5                       # in characters
WARNING = 'too bad, you picked the slow algorithm :('

def pairs(seq):
    n = len(seq)
    for i in range(n):
        yield seq[i], seq[(i + 1) % n]

def allUniqueSort(s):
    if len(s) > LIMIT:
        print(WARNING)
        time.sleep(SLOW)
    srtStr = sorted(s)
    for (c1, c2) in pairs(srtStr):
        if c1 == c2:
            return False
    return True

def allUniqueSet(s):
    if len(s) < LIMIT:
        print(WARNING)
        time.sleep(SLOW)
```

```
        return True if len(set(s)) == len(s) else False

    def allUnique(s, strategy):
        return strategy(s)


    def main():
        while True:
            word = None
            while not word:
                word = input('Insert word (type quit to exit)> ')

                if word == 'quit':
                    print('bye')
                    return

                strategy_picked = None
                strategies = { '1': allUniqueSet, '2': allUniqueSort }
                while strategy_picked not in strategies.keys():
                    strategy_picked = input('Choose strategy: [1] Use a
    set, [2] Sort and pair> ')

                    try:
                        strategy = strategies[strategy_picked]
                        print('allUnique({}): {}'.format(word,
    allUnique(word, strategy)))
                    except KeyError as err:
                        print('Incorrect option: {}'.format(strategy_
    picked))
                print()


    if __name__ == '__main__':
        main()
```

Let's view a sample execution of strategy.py:

```
>>> python3 strategy.py
Insert word (type quit to exit)> balloon
Choose strategy: [1] Use a set, [2] Sort and pair> 1
allUnique(balloon): False

Insert word (type quit to exit)> balloon
Choose strategy: [1] Use a set, [2] Sort and pair> 2
too bad, you picked the slow algorithm :(
```

```
allUnique(balloon): False

Insert word (type quit to exit)> bye
Choose strategy: [1] Use a set, [2] Sort and pair> 1
too bad, you picked the slow algorithm :(
allUnique(bye): True

Insert word (type quit to exit)> bye
Choose strategy: [1] Use a set, [2] Sort and pair> 2
allUnique(bye): True

Insert word (type quit to exit)> h
Choose strategy: [1] Use a set, [2] Sort and pair> 1
too bad, you picked the slow algorithm :(
allUnique(h): True

Insert word (type quit to exit)> h
Choose strategy: [1] Use a set, [2] Sort and pair> 2
allUnique(h): False

Insert word (type quit to exit)> quit
bye
```

The first word (balloon) has more than five characters and not all of them are unique. In this case, both algorithms return the correct result (False) but allUniqueSort() is slower and the user is warned.

The second word (bye) has less than five characters and all characters are unique. Again, both algorithms return the expected result (True) but this time, allUniqueSet() is slower and the user is warned once more.

The last "word" (h) is a special case. While allUniqueSet() is slow, it handles it properly and returns the expected True. The algorithm allUniqueSort() returns a super quick but incorrect result. Can you find out why? Fix the allUniqueSort() algorithm as an exercise. You might want to forbid single character words, which I find perfectly fine (definitely better than returning an incorrect result).

Normally, the strategy that we want to use should not be picked by the user. The point of the strategy pattern is that it makes it possible to use different algorithms transparently. Change the code so that the faster algorithm is always picked.

There are two usual users of our code. One is the end user, who should be unaware of what's happening in the code, and to achieve that we can follow the tips given in the previous paragraph. Another possible category of users is the other developers. Assume that we want to create an API that will be used by the other developers. How can we keep them unaware of the strategy pattern? A tip is to think of encapsulating the two functions in a common class, for example, `AllUnique`. In this case, the other developers will just need to create an instance of `AllUnique` and execute a single method, for instance, `test()`. What needs to be done in this method?

Summary

In this chapter, we saw the Strategy design pattern. Strategy is generally used when we want to be able to use multiple solutions for the same problem transparently. There is no perfect algorithm for all input data and all cases, and by using Strategy, we can dynamically decide which algorithm to use in each case. In reality, we use the Strategy pattern when we want to get to an airport to catch a flight.

Python uses the Strategy pattern to let the client code decide how to sort the elements of a data structure. We saw an example of how to sort programming languages based on their TIOBE index ranking.

The use of the Strategy design pattern is not limited to the sorting domain. Encryption, compression, logging, and other domains that deal with resources use Strategy to provide different ways to filter data. Portability is another domain where Strategy is applicable. Simulations are yet another good candidate.

We saw how Python with its first-class functions simplifies the implementation of Strategy by implementing two different algorithms that check if all the characters in a word are unique.

In the final chapter of this book, we will cover the Template pattern, which is used to abstract the common parts of an algorithm to promote code reuse.

16
The Template Pattern

A key ingredient in writing good code is avoiding redundancy. In object-oriented programming (OOP), methods and functions are important tools that we can use to avoid writing redundant code. Remember the `sorted()` example in the previous chapter. The `sorted()` function is generic enough that it can be used to sort more than one data structure (lists, tuples, and namedtuples) using arbitrary keys. That's the definition of a good function.

Functions such as `sorted()` demonstrate the ideal case. In reality, we cannot always write 100 percent generic code. There are many algorithms that have some (but not all) common steps. A good example is breadth-first search (BFS) and depth-first search (DFS), two popular algorithms used in graph searching. Assume that we are asked to implement BFS and DFS in Python. Initially, we come up with two independent implementations (the `graph.py` file). The functions `bfs()` and `dfs()` return a tuple of `(True, path)` if a path between `start` and `end` exists, or `(False, path)` (in this case, `path` is empty) if a path does not exist:

```
def bfs(graph, start, end):
        path = []
        visited = [start]
        while visited:
                current = visited.pop(0)
                if current not in path:
                        path.append(current)
                        if current == end:
                                print(path)
                                return (True, path)
                        # skip vertices with no connections
                        if current not in graph:
                                continue
```

```
                visited = visited + graph[current]
        return (False, path)


def dfs(graph, start, end):
        path = []
        visited = [start]
        while visited:
                current = visited.pop(0)
                if current not in path:
                        path.append(current)
                        if current == end:
                                print(path)
                                return (True, path)
                        # skip vertices with no connections
                        if current not in graph:
                                continue
                visited = graph[current] + visited
        return (False, path)
```

Notice the similarities between the two algorithms. There is only one difference that is highlighted. All the rest of the parts are exactly the same. We'll get back to that in a moment.

Let's first test the algorithms using the graph provided by Wikimedia [j.mp/wikicities]. For simplicity, we will assume that the graph is directed. This means that we can only move one way; we can check how we can go from Frankfurt to Mannheim but not the other way around.

We can represent the directed graph using dict of list. Each city is a key in dict, and the contents of list are all the possible destinations starting from that city. Cities that are leafs (for example, Erfurt) just use an empty list (no destinations):

```
def main():
  graph = {
        'Frankfurt':   ['Mannheim', 'Wurzburg', 'Kassel'],
        'Mannheim': ['Karlsruhe'],
        'Karlsruhe':   ['Augsburg'],
        'Augsburg':   ['Munchen'],
        'Wurzburg':   ['Erfurt', 'Nurnberg'],
        'Nurnberg':   ['Stuttgart', 'Munchen'],
```

```
                'Kassel':          ['Munchen'],
            'Erfurt':          [],
            'Stuttgart':   [],
            'Munchen':    []
                }

    bfs_path = bfs(graph, 'Frankfurt', 'Nurnberg')
    dfs_path = dfs(graph, 'Frankfurt', 'Nurnberg')
    print('bfs Frankfurt-Nurnberg: {}'.format(bfs_path[1] if bfs_path[0]
else 'Not
            found'))
    print('dfs Frankfurt-Nurnberg: {}'.format(dfs_path[1] if dfs_path[0]
else 'Not
            found'))

    bfs_nopath = bfs(graph, 'Wurzburg', 'Kassel')
    print('bfs Wurzburg-Kassel: {}'.format(bfs_nopath[1] if bfs_
nopath[0] else
            'Not found'))
    dfs_nopath = dfs(graph, 'Wurzburg', 'Kassel')
    print('dfs Wurzburg-Kassel: {}'.format(dfs_nopath[1] if dfs_
nopath[0] else
            'Not found'))

if __name__ == '__main__':
    main()
```

The results are not very interesting from a quality point of view because DFS and BFS do not work well with weighted graphs (the weights are completely ignored). Better algorithms to work with weighted graphs are shortest-path first (Dijkstra's), Bellman-Ford, A*, and so forth. However, we still want our graph traversal to be the expected. What we expect as the output of the algorithms is a list of the cities that were visited while searching for the path from Frankfurt to Nurnberg. So let's take a look at the results.

```
>> python3 graph.py
bfs Frankfurt-Nurnberg: ['Frankfurt', 'Mannheim', 'Wurzburg', 'Kassel',
                            'Karlsruhe', 'Erfurt', 'Nurnberg']
dfs Frankfurt-Nurnberg: ['Frankfurt', 'Mannheim', 'Karlsruhe',
'Augsburg',
```

```
                          'Munchen', 'Wurzburg', 'Erfurt', 'Nurnberg']
bfs Wurzburg-Kassel: Not found
dfs Wurzburg-Kassel: Not found
```

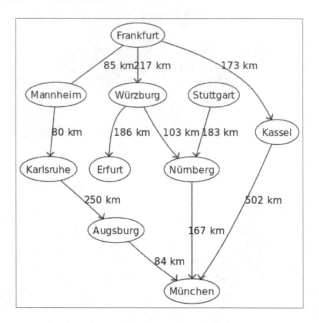

The results look fine. BFS traverses in breadth and DFS in depth, and both algorithms do not return any unexpected results. This is fine, but there is still a problem with our code: redundancy. There is only one difference between the two algorithms but the rest of the code is written twice. Can we do something about this problem?

The answer is yes. That's the problem solved by **The Template design pattern**. This pattern focuses on eliminating code redundancy. The idea is that we should be able to redefine certain parts of an algorithm without changing its structure. Let's see how the code looks after the necessary refactoring to avoid duplication (the `graph_template.py` file):

```
def traverse(graph, start, end, action):
    path = []
    visited = [start]
    while visited:
        current = visited.pop(0)
        if current not in path:
            path.append(current)
            if current == end:
                return (True, path)
            # skip vertices with no connections
```

```
                    if current not in graph:
                            continue
                visited = action(visited, graph[current])
        return (False, path)

def extend_bfs_path(visited, current):
    return visited + current

def extend_dfs_path(visited, current):
    return current + visited
```

Instead of having two `bfs()` and `dfs()` functions, we refactored the code to use a single `traverse()` function. The `traverse()` function is actually a Template function. It accepts `action` as a parameter, which is the function that "knows" how to extend the path. Depending on the algorithm that we use, we pass `extend_bfs_path()` or `extends_dfs_path()` as the action.

You might argue that we could achieve the same result by adding a condition inside `traverse()` to detect which traversal algorithm should be used. This is shown in the following code (the `graph_template_slower.py` file):

```
BFS = 1
DFS = 2


def traverse(graph, start, end, algorithm):
        path = []
        visited = [start]
        while visited:
                current = visited.pop(0)
                if current not in path:
                        path.append(current)
                        if current == end:
                                return (True, path)
                        # skip vertices with no connections
                        if current not in graph:
                                continue
                if algorithm == BFS:
                    visited = extend_bfs_path(visited, graph[current])
                elif algorithm == DFS:
                    visited = extend_dfs_path(visited, graph[current])
                else:
                    raise ValueError("No such algorithm.")
        return (False, path)
```

I don't like this solution for many reasons, as follows:

- It makes `traverse()` hard to maintain. If we add a third way to extend the path, we would need to extend the code of `traverse()` by adding one more condition to check if the new path extension action is used. It is better if `traverse()` acts like it has no idea about which `action` it should execute. No special logic in `traverse()` is required.

- It only works for algorithms that have one-line differences. If there are more differences, we are much better off creating a new function instead of polluting the `traverse()` function with details specific to `action`.

- It makes `traverse()` slower. That's because every time `traverse()` is executed, it needs to check explicitly which traversal function should be executed.

Executing `traverse()` is not very different from executing `dfs()` or `bfs()`. Here's an example:

```
bfs_path = traverse(graph, 'Frankfurt', 'Nurnberg', extend_bfs_path)
dfs_path = traverse(graph, 'Frankfurt', 'Nurnberg', extend_dfs_path)
print('bfs Frankfurt-Nurnberg: {}'.format(bfs_path[1] if bfs_path[0]
else 'Not
        found'))
print('dfs Frankfurt-Nurnberg: {}'.format(dfs_path[1] if dfs_path[0]
else 'Not
        found'))
```

The execution of `graph-template.py` should give the same results as the execution of `graph.py`:

```
>> python3 graph-template.py
bfs Frankfurt-Nurnberg: ['Frankfurt', 'Mannheim', 'Wurzburg', 'Kassel',
                         'Karlsruhe', 'Erfurt', 'Nurnberg']
dfs Frankfurt-Nurnberg: ['Frankfurt', 'Mannheim', 'Karlsruhe',
'Augsburg',
                  'Munchen', 'Wurzburg', 'Erfurt', 'Nurnberg']
bfs Wurzburg-Kassel: Not found
dfs Wurzburg-Kassel: Not found
```

A real-life example

The daily routine of a worker, especially for workers of the same company, is very close to the Template design pattern. All workers follow more or less the same routine, but specific parts of the routine are very different. This is shown in the following figure, provided by www.sourcemaking.com [j.mp/templatepat]. The fundamental difference between what is shown in the figure and implementing the Template pattern in Python is that in Python, inheritance is not mandatory. We can use it if it really benefits us. If there's no real benefit, we can skip it and use naming and typing conventions.

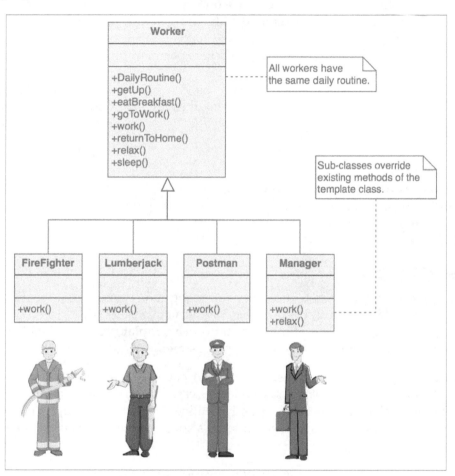

A software example

Python uses the Template pattern in the `cmd` module, which is used to build line-oriented command interpreters. Specifically, `cmd.Cmd.cmdloop()` implements an algorithm that reads input commands continuously and dispatches them to action methods. What is done before the loop, after the loop, and the command parsing part are always the same. This is also called the invariant part of an algorithm. What changes are the actual action methods (the variant part) [j.mp/templatemart, page 27].

The Python module `asyncore`, which is used to implement asynchronous socket service client/servers, also uses Template. Methods such as `asyncore.dispather.handle_connect_event()` and `asyncore.dispather.handle_write_event()` contain only generic code. To execute the socket-specific code, they execute the `handle_connect()` method. Note that what is executed is `handle_connect()` of a specific socket, not `asyncore.dispatcher.handle_connect()`, which actually contains only a warning. We can see that using the `inspect` module:

```
>> python3
import inspect
import asyncore
inspect.getsource(asyncore.dispatcher.handle_connect)
"    def handle_connect(self):\n        self.log_info('unhandled connect
event', 'warning')\n"
```

Use cases

The Template design pattern focuses on eliminating code repetition. If we notice that there is repeatable code in algorithms that have structural similarities, we can keep the invariant (common) parts of the algorithms in a template method/function and move the variant (different) parts in action/hook methods/functions.

Pagination is a good use case to use Template. A pagination algorithm can be split into an abstract (invariant) part and a concrete (variant) part. The invariant part takes care of things such as the maximum number of lines/page. The variant part contains functionality to show the header and footer of a specific page that is paginated [j.mp/templatemart, page 10].

All application frameworks make use of some form of the Template pattern. When we use a framework to create a graphical application, we usually inherit from a class and implement our custom behavior. However, before this, a Template method is usually called that implements the part of the application that is always the same, which is drawing the screen, handling the event loop, resizing and centralizing the window, and so on [EckelPython, page 143].

Implementation

In this section, we will implement a banner generator. The idea is rather simple. We want to send some text to a function, and the function should generate a banner containing the text. Banners have some sort of style, for example, dots or dashes surrounding the text. The banner generator has a default style, but we should be able to provide our own style.

The function `generate_banner()` is our Template function. It accepts, as an input, the text (`msg`) that we want our banner to contain, and optionally the style (`style`) that we want to use. The default style is `dots_style`, which we will see in a moment. The `generate_banner()` function wraps the styled text with a simple header and footer. In reality, the header and footer can be much more complex, but nothing forbids us from calling functions that can do the header and footer generations instead of just printing simple strings:

```
def generate_banner(msg, style=dots_style):
    print('-- start of banner --')
    print(style(msg))
    print('-- end of banner --\n\n')
```

The default `dots_style()` simply capitalizes `msg` and prints 10 dots before and after it:

```
def dots_style(msg):
    msg = msg.capitalize()
    msg = '.' * 10 + msg + '.' * 10
    return msg
```

Another style that is supported by the generator is `admire_style()`. This style shows the text in upper case and puts an exclamation mark between each character of the text:

```
def admire_style(msg):
    msg = msg.upper()
    return '!'.join(msg)
```

The next style is by far my favorite. The `cow_style()` style uses the `cowpy` module to generate random ASCII art characters emoting the text in question [j.mp/pycowpy]. If `cowpy` is not already installed on your system, you can install it using the following command:

```
>> pip3 install cowpy
```

The `cow_style()` style executes the `milk_random_cow()` method of `cowpy`, which is used to generate a random ASCII art character every time `cow_style()` is executed:

```python
def cow_style(msg):

    msg = cow.milk_random_cow(msg)
    return msg
```

The `main()` function sends the text "happy coding" to the banner and prints it to the standard output using all the available styles:

```python
def main():
    msg = 'happy coding'
    [generate_banner(msg, style) for style in (dots_style, admire_
style,
        cow_style)]
```

The following is the full code of `template.py`:

```python
from cowpy import cow

def dots_style(msg):
    msg = msg.capitalize()
    msg = '.' * 10 + msg + '.' * 10
    return msg

def admire_style(msg):
    msg = msg.upper()
    return '!'.join(msg)

def cow_style(msg):

    msg = cow.milk_random_cow(msg)
    return msg

def generate_banner(msg, style=dots_style):
    print('-- start of banner --')
    print(style(msg))
    print('-- end of banner --\n\n')

def main():
    msg = 'happy coding'
```

```
    [generate_banner(msg, style) for style in (dots_style, admire_
style, cow_style)]

if __name__ == '__main__':
    main()
```

Let's take a look at a sample output of `template.py`. Your `cow_style()` output might be different due to the randomness of `cowpy`:

```
>>> python3 template.py
-- start of banner --
.........Happy coding.........
-- end of banner --


-- start of banner --
H!A!P!P!Y! !C!O!D!I!N!G
-- end of banner --


-- start of banner --

 _____
< Happy coding >
 ---------------
  \
   \   \_\_    _/_/
    \      \__/
       (xx)_____
       (__)\        )\/\
        U   ||----w |
            ||      ||
-- end of banner --
```

Do you like the art generated by `cowpy`? I certainly do. As an exercise, you can create your own style and add it to the banner generator.

Another good exercise is to try implementing your own Template example. Find some existing redundant code that you wrote and the Template pattern is applicable. If you cannot find any good examples in your own code, you can still search on GitHub or any other code-hosting service. After finding a good candidate, refactor the code to use Template and eliminate duplication.

Summary

In this chapter, we covered the Template design pattern. We use Template to eliminate redundant code when implementing algorithms with structural similarities. The code duplication elimination happens using action/hook methods/ functions, which are first-class citizens in Python. We saw an actual example of code refactoring using the Template pattern with the BFS and DFS algorithms.

We saw how the daily routine of a worker resembles the Template pattern. We also mentioned two examples of how Python uses Template in its libraries. General use cases of when to use Template were also mentioned.

We concluded the chapter by implementing a banner generator, which uses a Template function to implement custom text styles.

This is the end of this book. I hope you enjoyed it. Before I leave you, I want to remind you about something by quoting Alex Martelli, an important Python contributor, who says, "Design patterns are discovered, not invented" [j.mp/templatemart, page 25].

Index

Thank you for buying
Mastering Python Design Patterns

About Packt Publishing

Packt, pronounced 'packed', published its first book, *Mastering phpMyAdmin for Effective MySQL Management*, in April 2004, and subsequently continued to specialize in publishing highly focused books on specific technologies and solutions.

Our books and publications share the experiences of your fellow IT professionals in adapting and customizing today's systems, applications, and frameworks. Our solution-based books give you the knowledge and power to customize the software and technologies you're using to get the job done. Packt books are more specific and less general than the IT books you have seen in the past. Our unique business model allows us to bring you more focused information, giving you more of what you need to know, and less of what you don't.

Packt is a modern yet unique publishing company that focuses on producing quality, cutting-edge books for communities of developers, administrators, and newbies alike. For more information, please visit our website at www.packtpub.com.

About Packt Open Source

In 2010, Packt launched two new brands, Packt Open Source and Packt Enterprise, in order to continue its focus on specialization. This book is part of the Packt Open Source brand, home to books published on software built around open source licenses, and offering information to anybody from advanced developers to budding web designers. The Open Source brand also runs Packt's Open Source Royalty Scheme, by which Packt gives a royalty to each open source project about whose software a book is sold.

Writing for Packt

We welcome all inquiries from people who are interested in authoring. Book proposals should be sent to author@packtpub.com. If your book idea is still at an early stage and you would like to discuss it first before writing a formal book proposal, then please contact us; one of our commissioning editors will get in touch with you.

We're not just looking for published authors; if you have strong technical skills but no writing experience, our experienced editors can help you develop a writing career, or simply get some additional reward for your expertise.

Learning Python Design Patterns

A practical and fast-paced guide exploring Python design patterns

Gennadiy Zlobin

PACKT open source *

Learning Python Design Patterns

ISBN: 978-1-78328-337-8   Paperback: 100 pages

A practical and fast-paced guide exploring Python design patterns

1. Explore the Model-View-Controller pattern and learn how to build a URL shortening service.

2. All design patterns use a real-world example that can be modified and applied in your software.

3. No unnecessary theory! The book consists of only the fundamental knowledge that you need to know.

Mastering Object-oriented Python

Grasp the intricacies of object-oriented programming in Python in order to efficiently build powerful real-world applications

Steven F. Lott

PACKT open source *

Mastering Object-oriented Python

ISBN: 978-1-78328-097-1   Paperback: 634 pages

Grasp the intricacies of object-oriented programming in Python in order to efficiently build powerful real-world applications

1. Create applications with flexible logging, powerful configuration and command-line options, automated unit tests, and good documentation.

2. Use the Python special methods to integrate seamlessly with built-in features and the standard library.

3. Design classes to support object persistence in JSON, YAML, Pickle, CSV, XML, Shelve, and SQL.

Please check **www.PacktPub.com** for information on our titles

Python for Secret Agents

ISBN: 978-1-78398-042-0   Paperback: 216 pages

Analyze, encrypt, and uncover intelligence data using Python, the essential tool for all aspiring secret agents

1. Build a toolbox of Python gadgets for password recovery, currency conversion, and civic data hacking.

2. Use stenography to hide secret messages in images.

3. Get to grips with geocoding to find villains' secret lairs.

Python Network Programming Cookbook

ISBN: 978-1-84951-346-3   Paperback: 234 pages

Over 70 detailed recipes to develop practical solutions for a wide range of real-world network programming tasks

1. Demonstrates how to write various besopke client/server networking applications using standard and popular third-party Python libraries.

2. Learn how to develop client programs for networking protocols such as HTTP/HTTPS, SMTP, POP3, FTP, CGI, XML-RPC, SOAP, and REST.

3. Provides practical, hands-on recipes combined with short and concise explanations on code snippets.

CPSIA information can be obtained
at www.ICGtesting.com
Printed in the USA
LVHW03s0044170818
587267LV00006B/44/P

9 781783 989324